D0070121

How to Look Like a Dancer

(*without being one*)

Alida Belair

MJF BOOKS
NEW YORK

Published by MJF Books
Fine Communications
322 Eighth Avenue
New York, NY 10001

How to Look Like a Dancer (without being one)
LC Control Number 2006939986
ISBN-13: 978-1-56731-866-1
ISBN-10: 1-56731-866-5

This edition is published by MJF Books in arrangement with Black Inc. Books.

Printed in the United States of America.

MJF Books and the MJF colophon are trademarks of Fine Creative Media, Inc.

QM 10 9 8 7 6 5 4 3 2 1

Contents

Preface

Over the 50-plus years that I have been involved in the world of dance and movement, both as a principal ballerina and a teacher, I have consistently explored a wide range of exercise disciplines as well as endeavoring to keep abreast of scientific advancements in movement philosophy, sports biomechanics, and indeed any new ideas about how the brain and the body interact.

Professional dancers have, by necessity, always been cross trainers. They are required to master an enormous range of skills that involve using different muscle groups and body parts all at once. Many sports, on the other hand, require the use of only a limited range of muscle groups and right-angle movements. Anything that enhances a dancer's athletic prowess is enthusiastically adopted, such as Pilates with its focus on core stability and alignment.

When I retired from the stage, I found myself thinking that classically trained dancers still epitomized athleticism at its best, despite the plethora of fitness fads available that promise miracle quick fixes. In my first book, *Travel Pilates*, I designed a fitness program to help Pilates devotees maintain their physical and mental well-being when they are away from the studio. Its focus was therefore on Pilates principles, albeit with my own slant. However, it seemed logical that a well-constructed program combining the proven traditions of classical dance and modern body-conditioning techniques would be the definitive workout.

Why Dance?

There are very sound reasons for developing a whole body workout based on the classical dance framework. Dance is inherent in all of us. It is in our blood to move and be moved by movement. Even if we think of ourselves as klutzes, when we submit to music and dance, we feel as if we have tapped into the energy field of life itself.

Naturally, few of us imagine that we could be transformed into dazzling dancers with superb physiques by doing a few select exercises. After all, dancers appear to defy gravity as they leap, spin, and glide across the stage with an effortlessness that makes them seem born to it. But while it is true that artists are born and not made, it is also true that dancers are, quite simply, brilliant athletes. Recent international studies conducted across a wide range of sports have only confirmed what dancers have always known: in terms of speed, agility, strength, and endurance, they are unsurpassed.

How do dancers develop and maintain their bodies as streamlined precision instruments? And what possible relevance could this have to those of us who would like to be as fit as possible but have not been blessed with the grace, poise, or perfect proportions of a dancer? A perfect body is not the prerogative of all dancers, but is instead the result of absolute dedication to a discipline with a proven tradition at its heart. It is also a discipline flexible enough to incorporate new scientific expedients.

In *How To Look Like a Dancer*, I have remained faithful to the key components of the classical dancer's training whilst keeping in mind that people come in all shapes, sizes, ages, and degrees of fitness. I have also kept in mind that people wish to work out for all sorts of reasons, among them vanity, health, recreation, or to enhance their performance in other sporting activities. Dance skills are found in many sports such as football, boxing, and racquet games.

Any master chef will tell you that the secret to a culinary work of art is firstly to select the best ingredients, and secondly to achieve the right mix and balance of flavors. Designing an effective workout is no different. Too many exercise programs are either so mindless or arduous that people don't last the distance. Moreover, they tend to focus on a limited range of movements. Rather than concentrating exclusively on one part of the body with one specific purpose, such as toning the buttocks or bulking up the pectorals, *How To Look Like a Dancer* focuses instead on balancing the actions of the muscles and joints into coordinated movements.

If you follow the instructions with care, attention to detail, common sense, and above all patience, the results will bring about permanent and positive changes to your body. However, while physical fitness in itself creates confidence and a sense of well-being, the human body has an extraordinary vocabulary of movement. I am confident that this workout will encourage you to further explore this wonderfully rich language.

Warning

If you are pregnant or suffer from any illness or injury always seek medical advice before commencing any exercise program. The cardiovascular section should not be undertaken if you have high blood pressure or a cardiovascular condition. Common sense dictates that if you bruise easily the floor exercises may be contraindicated.

Be responsible for yourself while you work out. Only you can know your own body's strengths and weaknesses.

Remember that the photographs are there to demonstrate the ideal way to perform the exercises. No one expects you to be perfect straightaway. Always approach exercises conservatively, and modify things if you have to – for example, keep your turnout to a minimum if you are tight in the hips, or only raise your leg to 45 degrees if you don't have the strength or flexibility to lift it higher. It is also advisable to keep your jumps low until you have mastered the technique.

Benefits

This thoughtful dance-inspired workout is designed to:

- Promote core strength, strong lean thighs and arms, a toned waistline, and the perfect posture, grace, and poise of a dancer
- Heighten body awareness
- Help break down our propensity for right-angle movements
- Provide a sense of flow to everyday functioning
- Strengthen, stretch, and stabilize
- Increase lung capacity
- Improve your cardiovascular conditioning
- Oxygenate the blood to replenish cells and increase blood flow to the brain
- Reduce stress and fatigue
- Improve physical confidence
- Promote ease and efficiency of movement
- Improve proprioception (proprioceptors update the brain on the location of body parts in relation to each other)

Best of all, though *How To Look Like a Dancer* will not turn you into a dancer, it will bring out the dancer in you.

The Human Skeleton

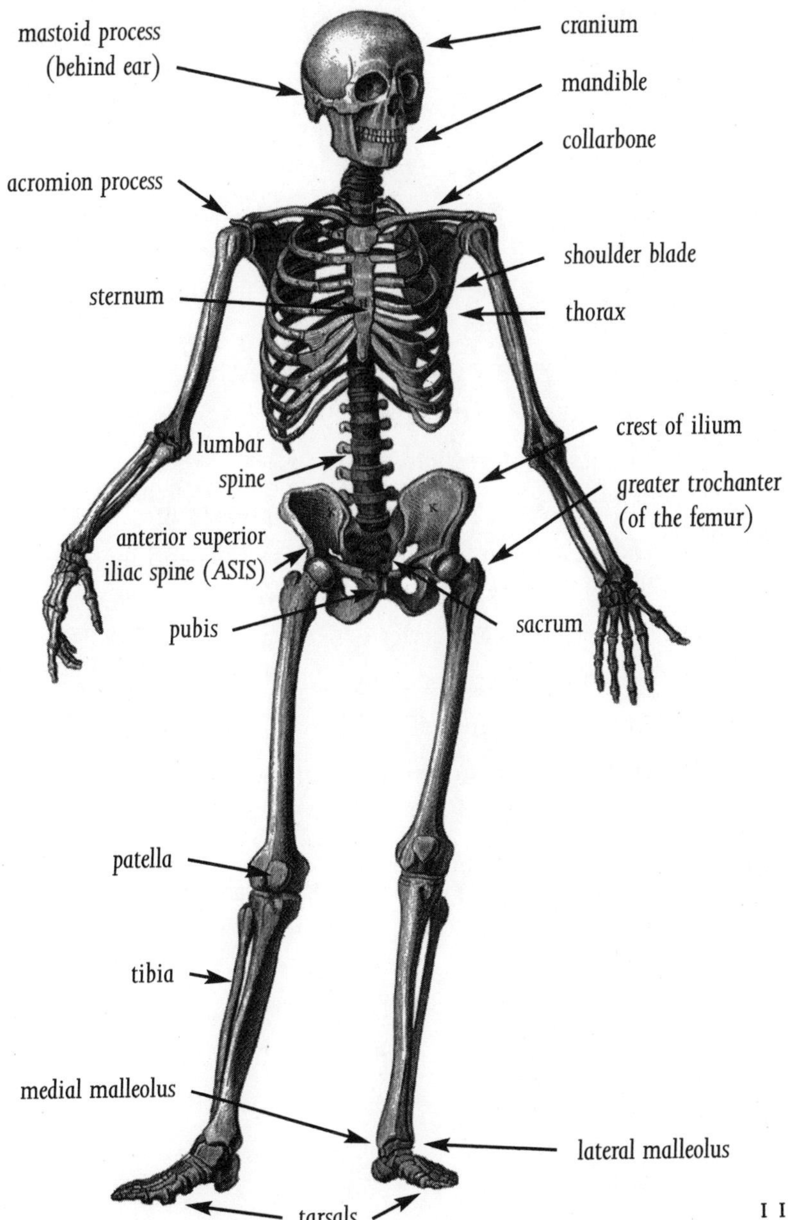

The Anterior Muscles of the Body

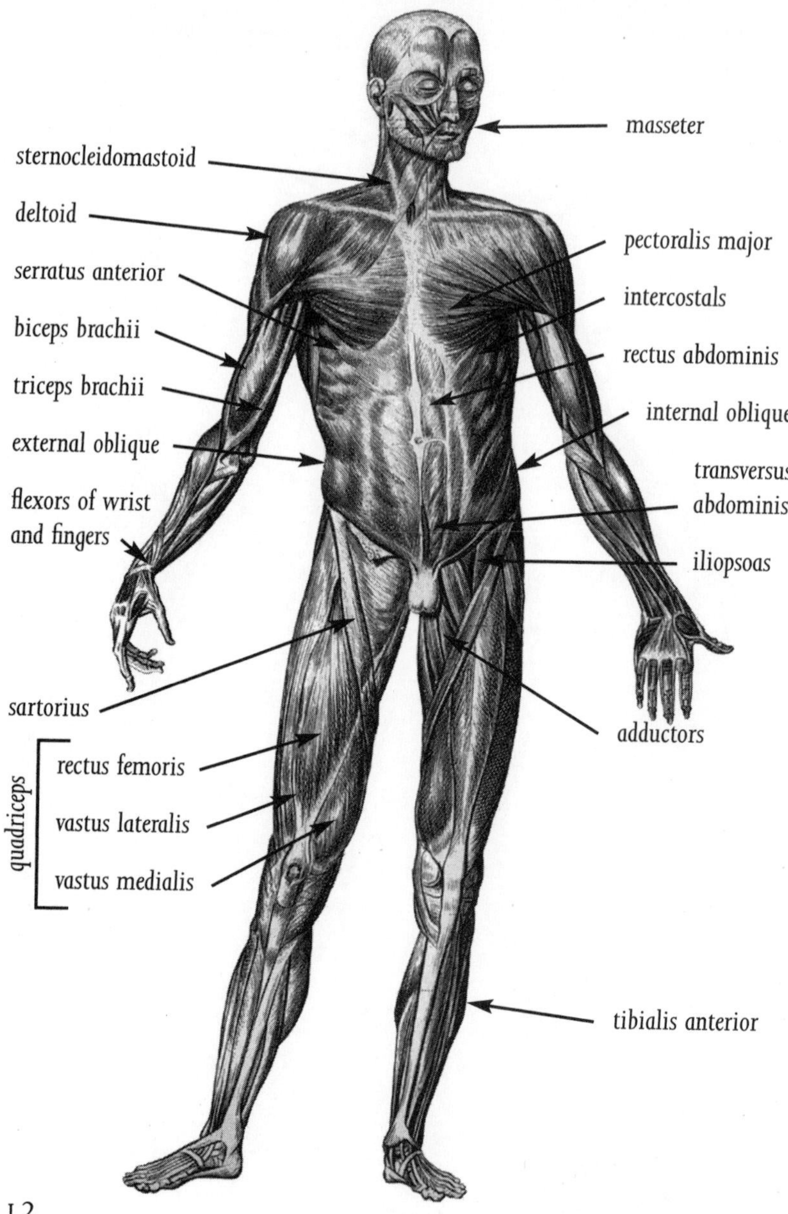

The Posterior Muscles of the Body

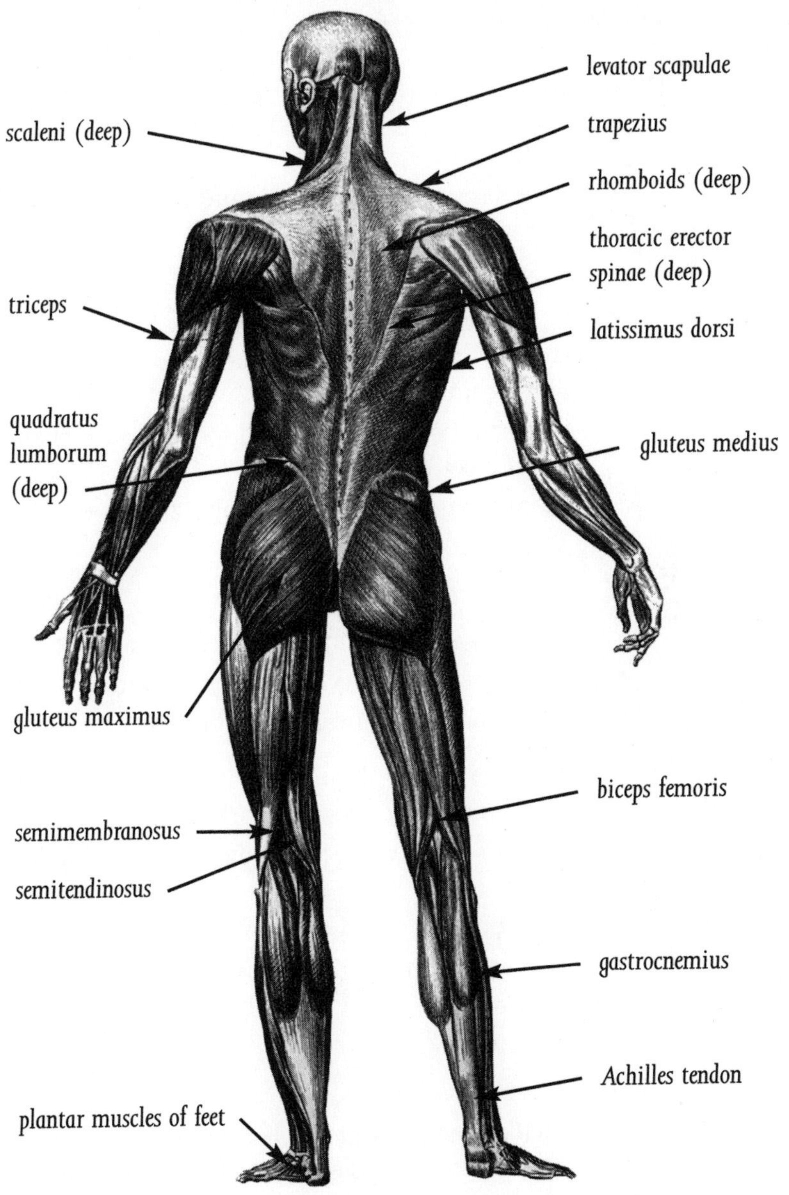

The Workout

The workout is comprised of the following sections:

1 Warm up

- Provides stretches to warm and loosen muscles and aid alignment

2 Floor work

- Enables you to target specific muscle groups around the body without having to concentrate on balance
- Prepares the body and mind for the more challenging center work
- Strengthens, stretches, and stabilizes

3 Center work

- Improves balance
- Improves coordination
- Heightens awareness of isolation and integration
- Strengthens, stretches, and stabilizes

4 Movement combination

- Provides a cardiovascular workout
- Enables you to work the body as an integrated whole
- Helps develop speed and agility
- Improves mental and physical agility through step combinations
- Helps release the dancer in you

5 Cooling down

- Provides deeper stretches to ease worked muscles back to a lengthened and loosened state

Getting Started

Plan to spend at least one hour, three times a week, on your workout – no excuses. No program works if you are not consistent.

Set the stage. You will need a quiet area with enough space to move around in comfortably. Remove objects that will get in the way. You don't want to be dodging around an armchair or tripping over the edge of a rug.

Wear something comfortable – natural fibers are best. Dancers usually begin with extra layers and then peel off item by item as their body warms up.

Footwear must be flexible enough to allow you to use all the muscles and bones of your foot, such as split-soled sneakers, ballet slippers or bare feet.

Eat lightly before your session. Digesting food while you work out can lead to cramps or indigestion. Drink water before and after your session.

As you step into your workout space, consciously **leave the outside world** behind. Ensure that your sessions are free of all distractions. This is *your* time. Insist on privacy if you are self-conscious, or work with a friend if you feel that it will make your session more enjoyable.

The power of **positive thinking** cannot be overestimated. Don't dwell on your deficiencies. This is where a sense of humor is a definite plus. Believe in your ability to change your body and you will be amazed at what you can achieve.

How To Use this Book

Although this progressive workout is most beneficial when it is done in its entirety, it can be modified to suit your daily requirements. Spend a few moments before you begin focusing on how your body feels. Are you tense in any specific area? If so, you may want to add a few more stretches targeting that area to your workout. Or if your abdominals are feeling under-worked, you may choose to prioritize the abdominal section. Whether or not you decide to modify the workout, it must always begin with a warm up and finish by cooling down.

Work through the exercises systematically. Focus your mind on every task. Don't move on until you understand the essence of the exercise or exercise combination. Remember that you are working new muscles in a new method, and it will take time to accustom your mind and body. No exercise should ever be done just for the sake of getting through it – sloppy technique leads to injury. Start slowly, pay attention to form, master the mechanics, and then try to make the movements flow. If you move seamlessly from one exercise to the next, the benefit of the workout will be optimal.

Remember to stay within your own limits. Unless you have practiced it from an early age, do not force the legs into a 180-degree turnout – 45 degrees is sufficient. Listen to your body and be conscious of the fine line between challenging your body and overdoing it.

Warm Up

Don't even think of moving your body through space without a warm up. Your muscles must be warm and loosened in order to stretch and respond efficiently, the joints need to be lubricated and mobilized, and the heart rate slightly elevated. This will help to prevent any sudden strain or injury.

Begin with the upper body and work down, so that the whole body is prepared.

Posture

The first thing to do is make sure your posture is correct. Posture is the mainstay of structural balance. Very few people realize that almost every part of the body is involved in simply standing upright, and that correct alignment must be carried through into everything else you do; sitting, walking, running, and of course exercising. Exercise an asymmetrical body in a random fashion and you are likely to do more damage than good.

Standing correctly is an exercise in itself. Practice in front of the mirror.

Stand with your feet parallel, hip-width apart. Let your arms rest by your sides. The plumb line runs from the crown of your head to just behind the metatarsals, with most of your weight falling between your first and second toes. You should be able to lift your heels off the floor without having to transfer your weight. Settling down onto your heels overloads the lumbar spine. Recruit your transversus abdominis, and lift the pelvic floor.

Slide your shoulder blades down your back and draw them into a V. The shoulder blade muscles support your upper spine. Hold your shoulders in a wide position, and open your chest. Keep your lower back in neutral. If the top of the pelvis tips forward, the lumbar curve increases. If it tips back, the lumbar spine flattens. Neutral is the position between the two extremes.

Lengthen up through your spine and neck. Do not push your head back or let it drop forward. Strike a balance between feeling pulled upward and relaxed at the same time. Control and focus is not synonymous with tension.

Remember, the way you stand and move reflects the level of your structural fitness and body balance.

Shoulder Circles

Mobility at the shoulder joints is easily lost, and tension in the shoulder area can have an adverse effect on your entire posture. Lack of use can stiffen the joints, whereas overuse is one cause of frozen shoulder.

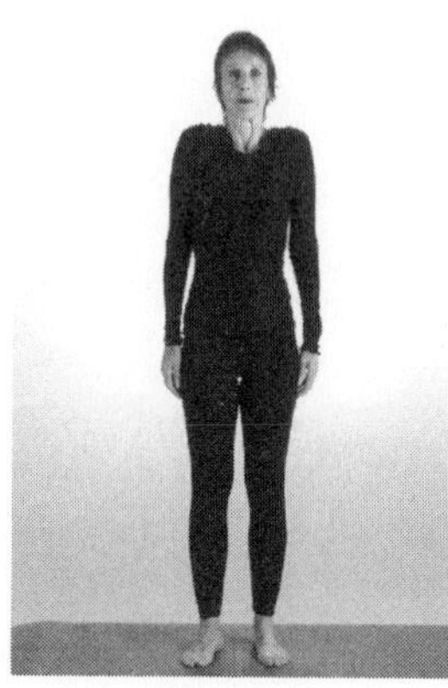

Stand with your feet parallel, hip-width apart, arms relaxed by your sides.

Circle your shoulders toward the back. Inhale as you lift the shoulders.

Exhale as you rotate the shoulders.

[10 reps]

Circle your shoulders toward the front. Inhale as you lift the shoulders.

Exhale as you rotate the shoulders.

[10 reps]

Isolate the movement to the shoulders, holding the arms still. Keep the rest of the trunk absolutely stable.

NECK & SHOULDER STRETCHES

These stretches help release tension in both the neck and shoulders.

For this sequence of stretches, stand with your feet parallel, hip-width apart, and relax your arms by your sides before you begin each stretch. When you finish one stretch, aim to move seamlessly on to the next.

Exercise 1

Inhale. Press the fingers of your right hand together, and place your palm at the side of your head just above the ear. Direct your elbow to the side. Pull your shoulder blades down your back.

Exhale. Press your head against your hand and resist its pressure. Hold for 6 seconds.

Relax and lower your hand back to your thigh.

Change hands and repeat.

[2 reps each side]

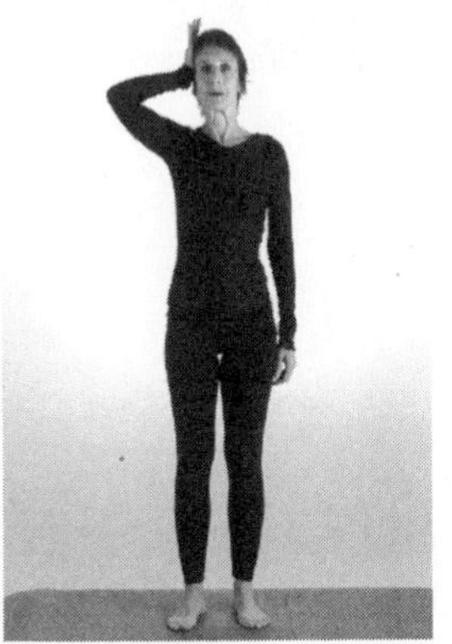

Exercise 2

Inhale. Place your right palm against your forehead, and direct your right elbow to the side. Pull your shoulder blades down your back.

Exhale. Press your forehead against your hand, resisting with your fingers. Hold for 6 seconds. Keep lengthening through your neck.

Relax and lower your hand back to your thigh.

Change hands and repeat.

[2 reps each side]

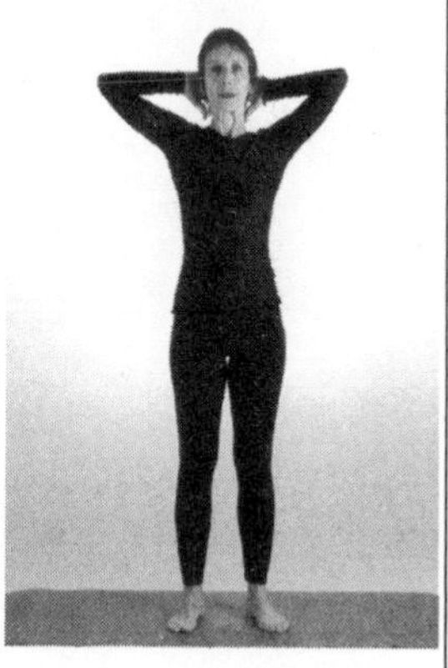

Exercise 3

Place the fingertips of both hands together, palms facing. Raise your arms overhead and place your hands in the hollow at the back of your neck. Direct your elbows to the side.

Inhale. Lengthen your spine and neck.

Exhale. Press your head gently back against your hands. Resist with your fingers. At the same time, pull your ribcage back toward your spine. Hold for 6 seconds. You should feel a lovely stretch down the spinal column.

Inhale.

Exhale. Lower your arms down to rest by your sides.

Repeat.

Exercise 4

Inhale. Incline your head to the left.

Exhale. Place your left hand on your right shoulder and gently push it down. Feel the stretch down the right side of the neck. Hold for 6 seconds.

Inhale.

Exhale. Straighten your neck and bring your arm down by your side.

Relax and change sides.

[2 reps each side]

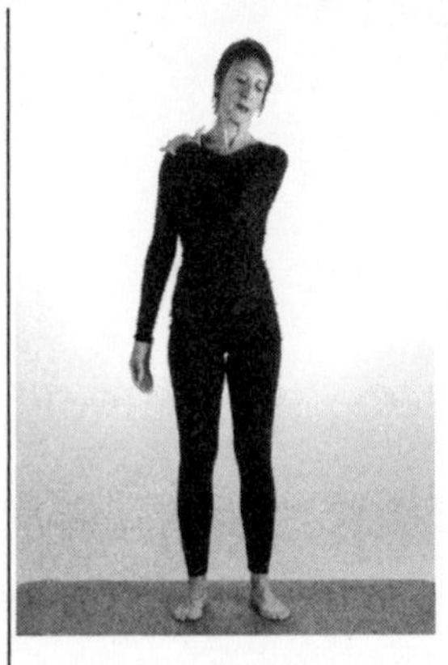

Exercise 5

Inhale. Incline your head to the left.

Exhale. Place your left hand on your right shoulder and gently push it down. Lift your right arm slightly away from your hip and flex the wrist. This will intensify the stretch at the neck, reaching into your arm. Hold for 6 seconds.

Relax and change sides.

[2 reps each side]

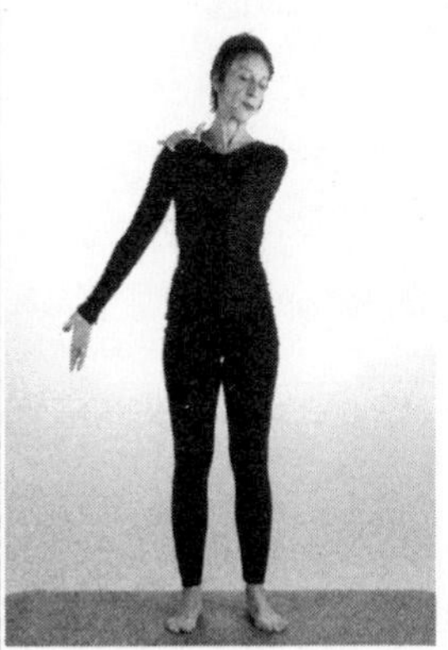

Arm Swings

This exercise will get the blood flowing and mobilize the spine, lower body, and shoulders.

Stand with your feet parallel, arms by your sides. Lengthen up through your spine, and keep your head aligned. Activate your transversus abdominis. Lift the pelvic floor.

Inhale. Raise your arms overhead. Be careful not to tilt the shoulders back. Keep your shoulder blades pulled down your back.

Exhale. Drop your chin toward your chest and roll down through your spine. Bend your knees and swing your arms behind you.

Inhale. Swing your arms forward and up overhead, straighten your knees and lengthen up through your spine, bone by bone. Move in a fluid rhythmic way.

[20 reps]

Climb a Rope

This exercise stretches the upper trunk muscles.

Stand with your feet parallel, hip-width apart, arms by your sides.

Inhale. Lift arms overhead.

Exhale. Raise your right hand and clasp an imaginary rope.

Inhale.

Exhale. Raise the left hand and take hold of the rope above the right hand.

Inhale.

[10 reps]

Lift your upper trunk out of the pelvic girdle and imagine that you are trying to split apart at the waist.

Exhale. Lower arms down to your sides and relax.

Épaulement

Épaulement means to turn the upper body $\frac{1}{8}$ away from the front. This rotating exercise mobilizes the spine and stretches the muscles of the upper and lower trunk and arms.

Stand with your feet parallel, hip-width apart, arms by your sides.

Inhale. Lift your arms to the front just below chest height.

Exhale. Open your arms to the side. Keep your elbows soft.

Inhale. Lengthen your spine and pull up out of the hips.

Exhale. Rotate your upper body ⅛ to the left, keeping both arms in line with your shoulders. Rotate arms with the body. Your right hand should be stretching away to the left corner with your left hand pulling in the opposite direction. Your head and eyes follow the right hand. Try to make a straight line from the fingers of the right hand to the fingers of the left. Feel the stretch across the shoulder blades.

Inhale. Return the upper body to the front.

Exhale. Rotate the upper body to the right and repeat the stretch on this side.

[8 reps alternating sides]

BIRD WINGS

This exercise integrates the movements of the muscles of the shoulder girdle. It also mobilizes the wrists and shoulders, and stretches the hands and arms.

Stand with your feet parallel, hip-width apart, arms by your sides.

Inhale. Lift arms overhead, leading from the wrists with fingers pointing toward the floor.

Bring the back of your wrists together, keeping the arms long and elbows soft. Slide your shoulder blades down your back.

Exhale. Lower your arms, leading with the front of the wrists, fingers pointing upward. To create resistance for the arm muscles, imagine you are pushing down a heavy body of water.

[10 reps]

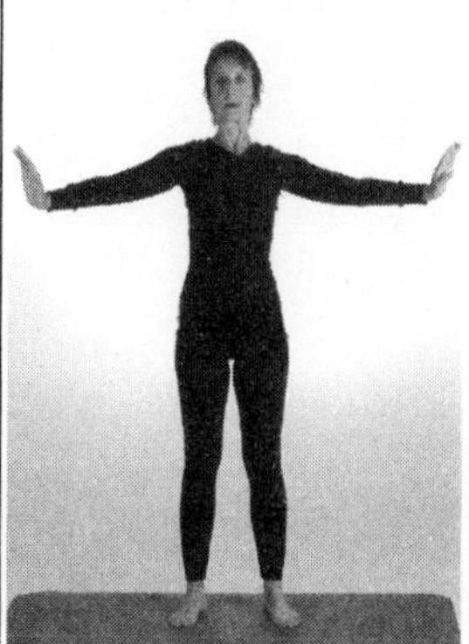

FLYING

This stretch mobilizes and strengthens the upper back and chest, and develops a sense of the integration and isolation of muscle groups.

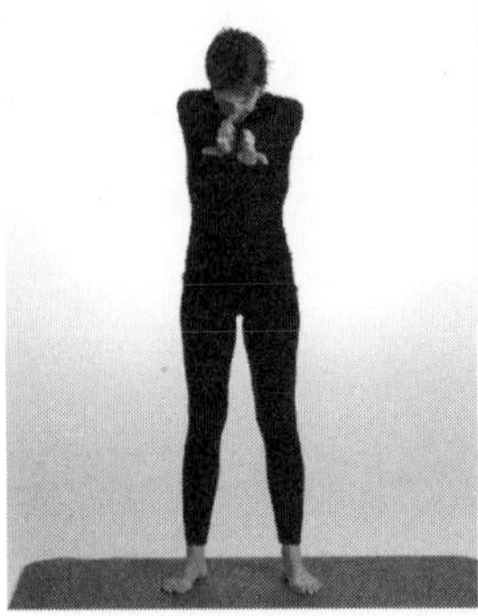

Stand with your feet parallel, hip-width apart, arms stretched to the side at just below shoulder level.

Inhale. Bring the arms forward, isolating and contracting the chest so that it becomes concave. The back of wrists should come together in line with the sternum. The upper back, across the shoulder blades, will be in flexion. Stabilize and anchor the rest of the trunk.

Exhale. Flex the hands at the wrists, and lift your chest up toward the ceiling. Once again, imagine you are pushing against a heavy body of water and open your arms as far back as you can without arching the lower back. Remain perfectly still and anchored in the rest of your torso. Feel the stretch across the chest. Keep your head and neck in line with the curve of the upper back. Don't force it.

[10 reps]

Repeat the above exercise but this time turn the palms of your hands toward the ceiling. This intensifies the stretch.

[10 reps]

Foot & Ankle Exercises

These exercises help maintain the natural structure of the foot, and develop an awareness of working the foot through its full muscle range. They mobilize and strengthen the intrinsic muscles of the feet and ankles, preventing weak ankles and collapsed arches.

Stand with your feet parallel, hip-width apart, and relax your arms by your sides before you begin each of the following exercises. When you finish one exercise, aim to move seamlessly on to the next.

Foot cramps often occur when people are not used to pointing their feet, but this should ease with practice.

Exercise 1

Inhale. Place your right foot up on pointed toes.

Exhale. Roll down through the foot – toe, ball, heel.

Alternate feet.

[10 reps each side]

Exercise 2

Inhale. Lift your right foot off the floor. Place your pointed toes on the floor, without crunching them. Roll through onto the ball of the foot, and down onto the heel.

Exhale. Stroke the whole foot along the floor, consciously feeling every centimeter of the floor beneath your foot. Try to develop the same sensitivity in your toes as you have in your fingertips.

Alternate feet.

[10 reps each side]

Exercise 3

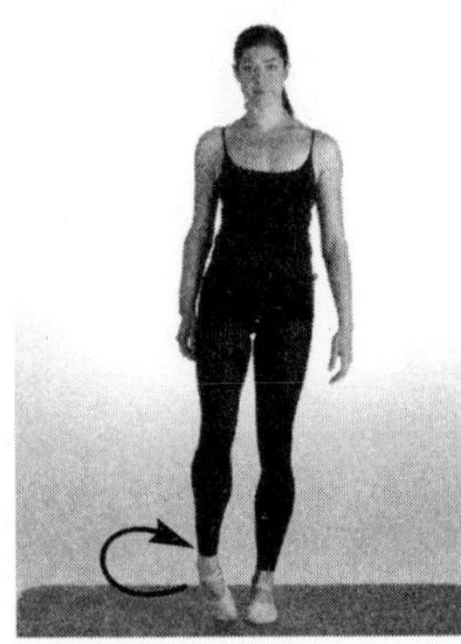

Inhale. Bend your right knee and rest your right foot lightly on pointed toes, without letting the toes curl.

Exhale. Isolating at the ankle muscles, rotate your foot.

[10 reps clockwise, 10 reps anticlockwise]

Change feet.

[10 reps clockwise, 10 reps anticlockwise]

With each rotation, exhale as you circle your ankle away from the center.

Calf Stretch

Normal activities such as walking cause your calf muscles to contract, so it's important that they are properly stretched in the warm up.

Stand with your feet together in parallel, knees straight, arms hanging loosely by your sides.

Inhale. Step forward with your right leg and transfer your weight onto the right foot, bending the knee directly over the toes. Stretch your back leg and lift the heel off the floor. Make sure that there is no weight on your back foot. There should be a straight line from your head to the heel of your left foot.

Keep your spine straight, abdominals recruited. Place your hands on your right thigh, just in front of the fold of the hip.

Exhale. Press your left heel down into the floor, keeping the knee straight and your weight over the right leg.

Inhale. Feel the calf stretch.

Exhale. Melt a little further into the stretch. Hold for 20–30 seconds.

Inhale. Straighten the right knee.

Exhale. Bring the left foot alongside the right.

Alternate sides.

[2 reps each side]

Hamstring & Lower Back Stretch

Tight hamstrings are common in people who spend long hours sitting every day. They can cause back pain and other problems.

Stand with your feet together in parallel, arms hanging loosely by your sides.

Inhale. Step back with your right leg and transfer your weight onto the right foot, bend your knee and keep it parallel to the opposite leg. Straighten your left leg, flex the foot and rest the heel on the floor. Place your hands at the fold of the hip of the right leg.

Exhale. Pitch the trunk forward from the hip flexor. Keeping your spine lengthened and straight, incline your forehead to the opposite wall. Feel the stretch in the lower back and right down the back of the leg.

Inhale.

Exhale. Melt further into the stretch without dropping the back. Hold for 20–30 seconds.

Inhale. Bring the back upright.

Exhale. Place the left foot back alongside the right.

Alternate sides.

[2 reps each side]

Iliopsoas & Quadriceps Stretch

This stretch targets the hip flexors and the muscles along the front of the thigh.

Take a lunge position, keeping the bent knee directly above the ankle.

Inhale. Lower the knee of the back leg to the floor with the foot directly behind it, and place your hands on the front thigh just above the knee.

Inhale. Recruit abdominals.

Exhale. Press hips forward and feel the stretch. Hold the stretch for 20–30 seconds.

Alternate sides.

[2 reps each side]

Lower Back Massage & Stretch

The twofold action of this stretch is especially good for loosening the muscles of the lower back.

Before you begin each of the following exercises, lie on your back with bent knees. Lift your feet off the floor, and place your hands on your knees.

When you finish one exercise, aim to move seamlessly on to the next.

Exercise 1

Inhale. Pull your knees towards your chest.

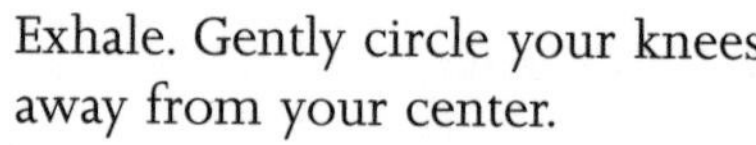

Exhale. Gently circle your knees away from your center.

[10 reps clockwise]

[10 reps anticlockwise]

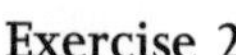

Exercise 2

Inhale.

Exhale. Place your hands on the left knee. Stretch your right leg along the floor with a pointed foot, simultaneously pulling the left knee up toward the chest.

Inhale. Bend the right knee back up towards the chest and place your right hand back on the right knee.

Exhale. Place your hands on the right knee. Stretch the left leg along the floor with a pointed foot, simultaneously pulling the right knee up toward the chest.

Inhale. Bend the left knee back up toward the chest and place your left hand back on the left knee.

[10 reps alternating sides]

The Cat

To undulate the spine and integrate the upper and lower spine.

Position yourself on all fours with your back neutral, hands directly under your shoulders, knees directly under your hips. Your head should float on a continuum with your spine.

Inhale.

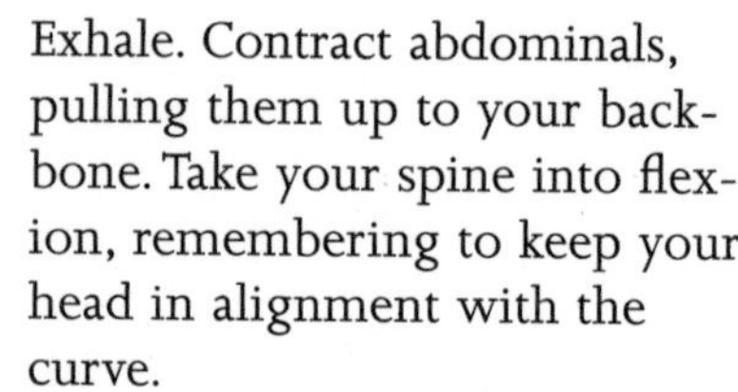

Exhale. Contract abdominals, pulling them up to your backbone. Take your spine into flexion, remembering to keep your head in alignment with the curve.

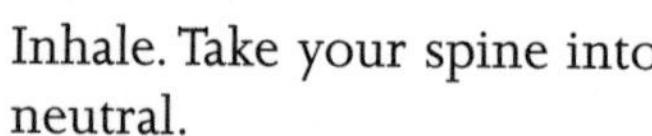

Inhale. Take your spine into neutral.

Exhale. Take your spine into extension. Bring the head up in line with the curve.

Inhale. Take your spine back to neutral.

[10 reps]

Exhale. Relax.

Floor Exercises

The purpose of this low impact section is to target specific groups of muscles without having to concentrate on balance, so that when you are doing your freestanding exercises you will have the strength and body awareness to use your body as effectively as possible.

You might want to place a mat or towel on the floor for this section.

Leg & Arm Stretches, Lying Prone

To develop core strength with the focus on centering and lengthening.

Begin the following exercises lying prone with the arms stretched overhead, legs straight and feet pointed.

Single Leg Stretch

Inhale.

Exhale. Recruit abdominals and imagine a metal plate under your lumbar spine as support. Lift the right arm and left leg, but do not lift too high. Think of lengthening and releasing the limbs from the joints rather than lifting. Keep both hips on the floor, and do not twist the torso or limbs. Your head should be slightly higher than the parallel of your arms.

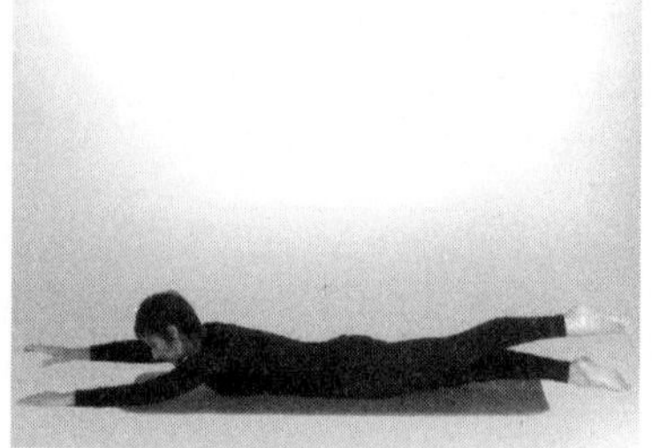

Inhale. Lower limbs and head to floor.

Exhale. Relax.

Change sides.

[10 reps alternating sides]

Double Arm & Leg Stretch

Inhale.

Exhale. Recruit abdominals and lift both arms and legs off the floor. Stretch away from your center in opposite directions. Think of stretching and releasing, rather than lifting.

Inhale. Lower limbs and head to floor.

Exhale. Relax.

[10 reps]

Upper Back Strengtheners

To mobilize and strengthen the upper to mid back.

Aim to move seamlessly from one exercise to the next in this section.

Exercise 1

Lie prone and place your hands at the nape of your neck, keeping your elbows wide and your shoulder blades pulled down your back. Your legs should be lengthening away from the center of your body, with the thighs squeezed together.

Inhale.

Exhale. Lift the head and shoulders off the floor, keeping the elbows wide. Only recruit the muscles in the upper to middle of the back. Imagine you are being pulled off the floor by a string attached from the middle of your shoulder blades to the ceiling.

Do not hyperextend at the neck. Keep the head and neck in line with your spine.

Inhale. Lower head and shoulders back to the floor.

Exhale.

[10 reps]

Exercise 2

Lie prone as above, but stretch your arms overhead.

Inhale.

Exhale. Lift head, shoulders, and arms off the floor. Keep the shoulder blades pulled down your back and do not recruit the muscles in the lower back.

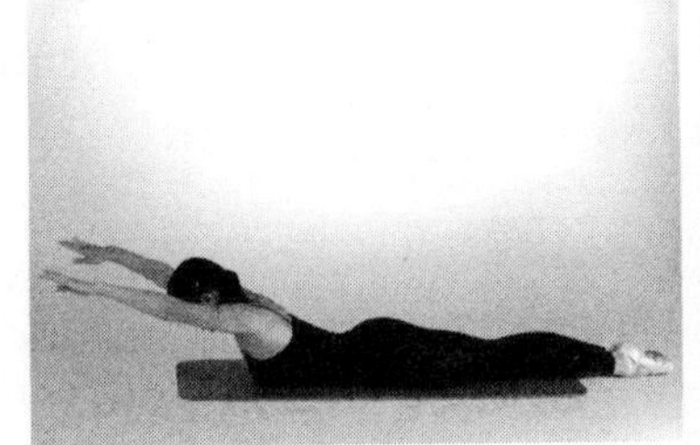

Inhale. Return your head, chest, and arms back to the floor.

Exhale.

[10 reps]

Leg Exercises

To work the hamstrings, glutei, and stabilize the pelvis.

Aim to move seamlessly from one exercise to the next in this section.

Exercise 1

Lie prone with your forehead on your hands, elbows directed to the side. Keep your legs together with your feet pointed.

Inhale.

Exhale. Raise your right leg off the floor. Think of lengthening and releasing the limb out of the hip joint rather than aiming for height.

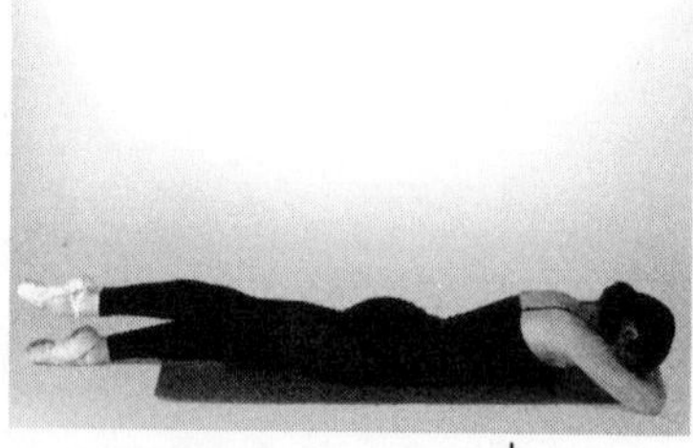

Inhale. Lower leg and foot back to the floor.

Exhale.

Alternate sides.

[10 reps]

Exercise 2

Lie prone with your forehead on your hands, elbows directed to the side. Keep your legs together with your feet pointed.

Inhale.

Exhale. Raise both legs off the floor, working them as one unit. Recruit your abdominals and keep your pelvis neutral. Be careful not to dip at the lumbar spine. Think of reaching away from your center and releasing the limbs out of the hip joints.

Exhale.

[10 reps]

Exercise 3

This exercise challenges the stability at the core while you move the upper and lower limbs in isolation.

Lie prone and stretch your arms overhead. Squeeze your upper inner thighs together, and point your toes.

Inhale.

Exhale. Lift both arms and legs off the floor, and stretch away from your center with your hands and toes pulling in opposite directions. Pull your navel up to your backbone.

Inhale.

Exhale. Sweep your arms outward and down to the sides of your trunk, keeping the elbows soft but lengthened. (If you want to engage the triceps, rotate the arms in the shoulder sockets to bring the elbows in close to the trunk.)

Inhale. Move the arms back overhead, keeping the arms long. The rest of the body should remain absolutely still and stabilized as you move the arms.

[10 reps]

Exhale. Don't come down. Keep engaging your abdominals. While you hold the arms still overhead, you will now move the legs in isolation.

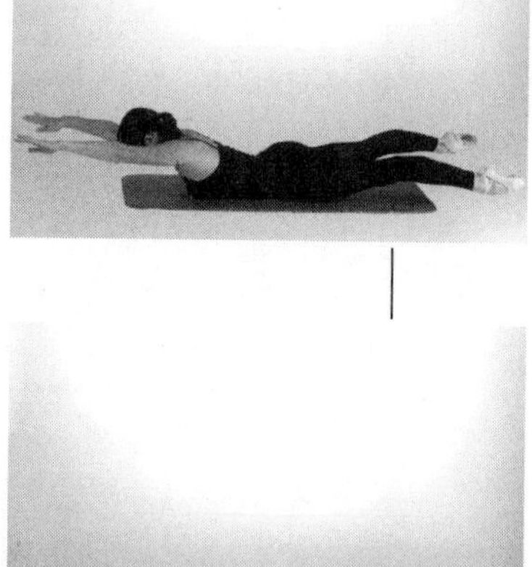

Inhale. Open the legs to the side with pointed feet.

Exhale. Flex your feet and draw your legs together, touching at the heels and thighs. Feel as if there is a magnetic force between your thighs, pulling them together.

[10 reps]

Inhale.

Exhale. Lower the limbs and head to the floor. Relax.

Waist-toning Exercises

To strengthen the abdominals, particularly the obliques, hips, buttocks, and leg muscles.

Aim to move seamlessly from one exercise to the next in this section.

Exercise 1

Lie on your right side with hips stacked on top of one another and rest your head on your outstretched arm. Use your left hand to gently support your body against the floor, preventing the body from rolling. (I like to think of this hand providing moral rather than actual support.)

Your back should be in neutral and your legs in line, toes pointing. However, if you feel your pelvis tilting forward, thereby taking the spine out of neutral, angle legs slightly forward at the hips.

Inhale. The spine is lengthened and parallel to floor.

Exhale. Initiate by engaging the waist muscles. Then lift the trunk and legs simultaneously so that your body is in line. Keep lengthening through the spine and along the back of the neck (the head should float on a continuum with the spine).

Watchpoints

Initiate at the waist first. Keep your shoulders down and shoulder blades pulled down your back – the back must be neutral. Keep eyes focused to the front.

Feel the muscles at the waist working.

Inhale. Lower the head, trunk and legs back down onto the floor and feel the waist muscles imprint the floor.

Exhale.

[10 reps]

When you are confident with the above, allow the upper arm to rest along the side of your body. Slide your hand down the side of your thigh as your body lifts – let your eyes follow the hand.

Exercise 2

Lie on your right side with your right elbow propped underneath you. Your elbow should be directly under your shoulder and your forearm at a right angle to your body. Keep your head aligned with your spine.

Place your legs on top of one another, keeping the hip bones vertically stacked. Angle your legs slightly to the front so that your spine can remain neutral. Rest your left hand on your thigh.

Inhale.

Exhale. Contract your abdominals and lift your pelvis off the floor. Your neck should remain in line with your spine. Make a straight line from the crown of the head to the toes.

Inhale. Lower your body back onto the floor.

Exhale.

[10 reps]

Exercise 3

Lie on your side as described above in Exercise 2.

Inhale.

Exhale. Contract your abdominals and lift your pelvis off the floor.

Inhale.

Pulse. Lift the left hip up towards the ceiling.

A pulse refers to a short exhalation.

Inhale. Bring the hip back in line with the rest of your body. Continue to lift the hip for 9 more pulses.

Inhale. Bring the hip back in line.

Exhale. Lower the pelvis to the floor.

Repeat Exercises 1 to 3 lying on your left side.

Pelvic Girdle & Thigh Exercises

These exercises stretch the quadratus lumborum and strengthen the leg abductor and adductor muscles, the pelvic girdle, the gluteus medius, and iliotibial tract.

Lie on your right side with hips stacked on top of each other and your head on your outstretched right arm. Aim to move seamlessly from one exercise to the next in this section.

Exercise 1

Inhale.

Exhale. Initiate by engaging the waist muscles. Then lift the trunk and legs simultaneously from the floor so that your body is in line.

Inhale.

Exhale. Lower your right leg to the floor.

Inhale. Raise the right leg off the floor towards the upper leg. Keep the pelvis neutral and your left leg to the height of the hip.

Exhale. Squeeze your thighs together.

Inhale. Hold that position.

Exhale. Lower the right leg back to the floor.

[6 reps]

Exercise 2

Stay in the same position as above, with the legs and trunk raised off the floor.

Inhale. Lower the right leg to the floor.

Exhale. Lift the right leg up to join the left leg, which is still held at hip height.

Inhale. Lower the right leg back to the floor.

[10 reps]

Stay in the same position, with the trunk and legs raised off the floor.

Inhale. Lift the left leg off the right leg.

Exhale. Lower the left leg to meet the right leg.

Inhale. Lift the left leg off the right leg, which is raised and stationary.

Exhale. Lower the left leg back onto the right leg. Squeeze your thighs together each time you join your legs. Keep the legs in line with your upper hip.

[10 reps]

Inhale.

Exhale. Lower your body to the floor.

Turn onto the other side and repeat both exercises.

Abdominal Exercises

It is a good idea to vary your abdominal exercises from time to time. This sharpens your focus and challenges your body in different ways. You should never exercise with your mind switched to automatic pilot.

Select a range of exercises from the following, but make sure that you strike a balance between the simple movements and the challenging ones. Aim to move seamlessly from one exercise to the next.

Exercises 1 and 2 are compulsory, so make sure you include these first in your chosen sequence.

Exercise 1

Lie on your back with your knees in constructive rest. Keep your spine neutral. Place hands at the back of your head just behind your ears, keeping elbows open to the side.

Inhale.

Exhale. Lift your head and shoulders, keeping the head aligned with the spine. You should be able to fit a tennis ball between your chin and clavicle. Use the xiphoid process at the base of the sternum as a fulcrum. Draw your abdominals in toward your navel, and keep your ribs anchored to the floor.

Visualize a weight pressing down on your trunk as you pluck your vertebrae off the floor, bone by bone. The more resistance you create with your abdominals, the stronger they will become.

Inhale. Roll the spine down to the floor, bone by bone.

Exhale.

[10 reps]

Exercise 2

Lie on your back with your knees in constructive rest. Keep your spine neutral. Place hands at the back of your head just behind your ears, keeping elbows open to the side.

Inhale.

Exhale. Lift your head and shoulders off the floor using the xiphoid process as a fulcrum, and scoop your abdominals.

Inhale. Release your scoop by 10 percent.

Exhale. Contract your abdominals again.

Inhale. Release by 10 percent.

Exhale.

[10 reps]

Exercise 3

Lie in the constructive rest position, arms down by your sides. Bend your knees and lift your feet off the floor so that the thighs are at a 90-degree angle to the floor.

Inhale.

Exhale. Peel your head and shoulders off the floor using the xiphoid process as a fulcrum. Keep your trunk anchored. Slide arms toward feet, parallel to the floor. Keep the shoulder girdle stabilized.

Inhale. Lower head, shoulders, and arms by rolling down the spine, bone by bone, to the floor.

Exhale.

[10 reps]

Exercise 4

Lie in the constructive rest position, arms down by your sides. Bend your knees and lift your feet off the floor so that the thighs are at a 90-degree angle to the floor.

Inhale.

Exhale. Peel your head and shoulders off the floor and on the tail end of the exhalation stretch your legs away from the center of your body. Keep the pelvis anchored. Do not fully stretch the legs if you feel the effort transferring into your lower back. Slide arms toward feet, parallel to the floor.

Inhale. Lower your head, shoulders, and arms to the floor.

Exhale.

[10 reps]

Exercise 5

Lie on your back in the constructive rest position, feet raised off the floor.

Place hands at the back of your head just behind your ears, keeping elbows open to the side.

Inhale.

Exhale. Straighten your legs toward the ceiling at a right angle to the floor. Make sure that your buttocks remain firmly on the floor and that your pelvis is neutral. If your hamstrings are too tight to allow you to fully stretch your legs, keep your knees bent, thighs at 90 degrees.

Inhale.

Exhale. Lift your head and shoulders off the floor and rotate your upper body to the right. At the same time, reach past the back of your right ankle with your left hand. If you are doing the bent knee version, lift your body and reach past the right knee with your left hand.

Inhale. Roll your spine to the floor, bone by bone, and place the hand back on the head.

Exhale. Lift your head and shoulders off the floor and rotate your upper body to the left, reaching past your left ankle or knee with the right hand.

Inhale. Roll down and return hand to head.

Exhale.

[10 reps]

Exercise 6

Lie with your legs raised at a right angle to the floor, keeping your knees as straight as you can. Place your hands at the back of your head, elbows wide.

Inhale. Lift your head and shoulders off the floor using the xiphoid process as a fulcrum. Keep ribs and pelvis anchored.

Exhale. Flex feet. Slowly lower your right leg toward the floor for 4 counts.

Inhale. Return right leg to vertical beside the left.

Exhale. Lower your left leg toward the floor for 4 counts.

Inhale. Return it to vertical beside the right.

[10 reps]

Exhale. Lower head and shoulders to the floor.

Exercise 7

Lie with your legs raised at a right angle to your hips, knees as straight as you can. Turn your legs out without forcing them. Place your hands at the back of the head with the elbows open to the side.

Inhale. Lift your head and shoulders off the floor using the xiphoid process as a fulcrum.

Next you will give 5 short exhalations on 5 beats. With each exhalation, slightly open the legs and close one foot over the other with a snapping motion, swapping the feet, while gradually lowering the legs towards the floor. Don't let the lower back lift off the floor. Keep the pelvis anchored.

Now take 5 inhalations on 5 beats. Swap the feet as above, but gradually lift the legs back up with each beat.

[10 reps]

Exhale. Lower legs, head, and shoulders to the floor. Relax.

Maintain the scoop at your abdominals throughout. If you feel this exercise in your back, don't lower your legs too much in the first beats. If you still feel discomfort, leave the exercise out.

Alternative or Additional Abdominal Exercises

To work the entire abdomen, the pelvic floor, and the arms and shoulders.

The following exercises can be completed in addition to those on pages 50–55, or for the sake of variety, can be substituted for Exercises 3–7.

Exercise 1

Sit up tall on your sitting bones, knees bent. Press your feet into the floor, and lengthen up through your spine.

Inhale. Place your palms together so that the back of one hand is towards you, and the other faces away. Round your arms.

Exhale. Press your palms together. Lift the pelvic floor, scoop the abdominals and leading with the coccyx, roll your vertebrae bone by bone, down towards the floor. Press down on your heels but curl the toes towards your body. When you have a good scoop, take a short breath in and release the pressure on the palms.

Maintain the scoop. Exhale for 6 seconds and press into the palms.

Take a short breath in. Release the pressure on the palms.

Exhale. Press the palms for 6 seconds.

Inhale. Release the palms.

Exhale. Press the palms for 6 seconds.

Inhale. Release the palms.

Exhale. Roll your vertebrae back on top of one another, bone by bone, starting with the coccyx, until you are sitting upright. Then stretch your arms forward past your knees, keeping the back straight. Focus on stretching the lower back muscles.

Reverse the hands, and repeat.

Exercise 2

Sit up tall on your sitting bones, knees bent. Press your feet into the floor, and lengthen up through your spine.

Inhale. Place your palms together as in Exercise 1 and round your arms.

Exhale. Press against your palms and roll down vertebrae by vertebrae towards the floor until you have created a good scoop.

Take a short inhalation. Release the pressure on the palms of your hand.

Exhale. Press into the palms for 6 seconds.

Inhale. Release the palms.

Exhale. Press the palms together.

Inhale. Release the palms.

Exhale. Press the palms together.

Inhale. Keeping the scoop at the abdominals and the palms pressed together, rotate your body to the right from the waist.

Exhale. Press the palms together for 6 seconds.

Inhale. Release the pressure.

Exhale. Press the palms together.

Inhale. Release the pressure.

Exhale. Press the palms together.

Inhale. Keeping the scoop at the abdominals, rotate the body to the left side for three slow exhalations and palm presses.

Inhale. Rotate the scooped body back to the center.

Exhale. Rebuild the spine, bone by bone, until you are sitting upright.

Now reach past your knees and stretch out your lower back, keeping the spine lengthened.

Exercise 3

Lie on your back with your legs turned out, knees bent and soles of your feet touching. Open your arms to the side at shoulder height.

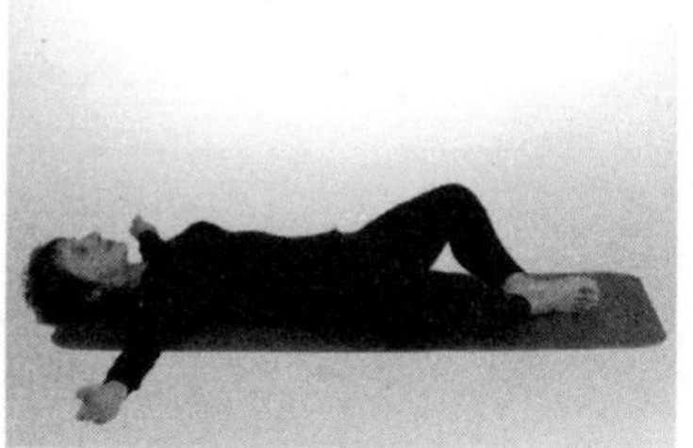

Inhale.

Exhale. Lift your head and shoulders off the floor, simultaneously closing your knees. Bring your arms and hands together in front of your body. Resist with your abdominals. Keep your arms parallel to the floor and stretch the hands as far beyond the knees as you can.

Inhale. Roll the head and shoulders to the floor bone by bone, simultaneously opening the arms and legs back to the starting position.

[10 reps]

Exhale.

Exercise 4

Now you will perform abdominal circles. Lie on your back in constructive rest, arms down by your sides.

Inhale.

Exhale. Lift your head, shoulders and arms off the floor while simultaneously rotating 45 degrees to the left. Keep the arms rounded in front of your body with the fingertips touching.

Inhale. Rotate body and arms to the center and reach. Keep lifting into the abdominals, which should be working hard in opposition.

Exhale. Rotate 45 degrees to the right, with your abdominals still resisting.

Inhale. Lower your body towards the floor with a circular movement, while releasing the muscles.

[6 reps]

Exhale.

Exercise 5

Now you will perform seamless abdominal circles.

Lie on your back in constructive rest, arms down by your sides.

Inhale.

Exhale. Lift and circle your head, shoulders and arms to the left at 45 degrees.

Inhale. Without stopping, circle to the center, the right and then down towards the floor **without** fully releasing the scoop.

[6 reps]

Exhale.

Repeat Exercises 4 and 5 anticlockwise.

Double Leg Kick

This exercise stretches the thigh and abdominal muscles, and strengthens the hamstrings, hip flexors, chest muscles, and arms.

Lie prone with your legs parallel. Clasp your hands in the small of your back.

Inhale. Bend your knees and lift them slightly off the floor.

With three small pulses (exhalations), beat the heels toward the buttocks.

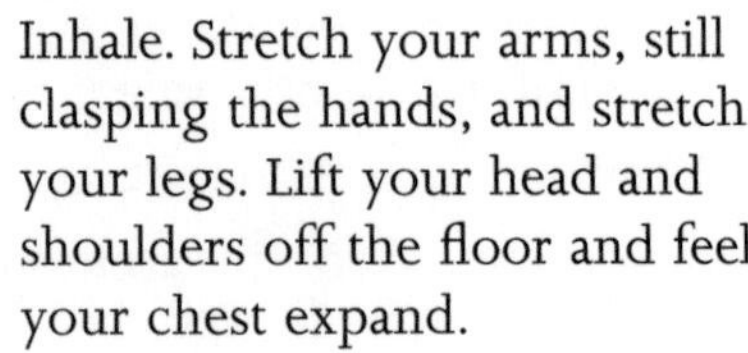

Inhale. Stretch your arms, still clasping the hands, and stretch your legs. Lift your head and shoulders off the floor and feel your chest expand.

Exhale. Lower your trunk, shoulders, and head back to the floor, and bend the knees.

[10 reps]

Exercises to Integrate the Upper & Lower Body

These exercises integrate the upper and lower body with a focus on core stability. Aim to move seamlessly from one exercise to the next.

Exercise 1

Lie on your back, legs in constructive rest, spine neutral. Place your hands behind your head with elbows held wide.

Inhale.

Exhale. Lift your head and shoulders off the floor while simultaneously lifting the right knee towards your chest.

Inhale. Return your foot to the floor while simultaneously rolling down your head and shoulders.

Exhale.

[8 reps, alternating legs]

Exercise 2

Lie on your back, legs in constructive rest, spine neutral. Place your hands behind your head with elbows held wide.

Inhale.

Exhale. Lift your head and shoulders off the floor, simultaneously lifting your right knee towards your chest.

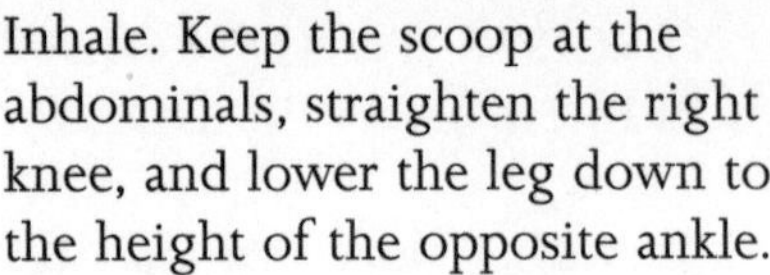

Inhale. Keep the scoop at the abdominals, straighten the right knee, and lower the leg down to the height of the opposite ankle.

Exhale. Keep the scoop, bend your knee, and lift it back towards your chest.

Inhale. Return your foot, head, and shoulders to the floor.

Exhale.

[8 reps, alternating legs]

Exercise 3

Lie on your back, legs in constructive rest, spine neutral. Place your hands behind your head with elbows held wide.

Inhale.

Exhale. Lift your head and shoulders off the floor, simultaneously lifting your right knee towards your chest.

Inhale. Straighten your right leg, lowering it to the height of your opposite ankle. At the same time, lower your head and shoulders to the floor with the arms opening to the side. Keep the connection at the abdominals.

Exhale. Bring your hands back to the head with elbows held wide, rotate your body and lift your head and shoulders off the floor towards the raised right bent leg. The more obtuse the knee angle at the raised leg, the higher you will need to lift the rotated upper body.

Inhale. Lower your head and shoulders back down to the floor, vertebra by vertebra, to constructive rest.

Exhale. Relax.

[8 reps, alternating legs]

Leg Exercises

To promote long, lean, and strong leg muscles.

For the following sequence of exercises, lie on your back with your knees bent and arms by your sides on the floor. Make certain that your back and pelvis are in a neutral position before you begin. Move seamlessly from one exercise to the next.

Exercise 1

Inhale. Recruit your abdominals. Lift your right foot off the floor and unfold your leg toward the ceiling, pointing your toes.

Exhale. Flex your foot and lower your straight leg toward the floor to the height of your opposite ankle. The movement should be controlled and flowing.

[8 reps]

Exercise 2

Inhale. Lift your right leg with a straight knee and flexed foot to a 90-degree angle with the body.

Exhale. Bend the knee, point your toes, and unfold the leg downwards to the height of the opposite ankle.

Inhale. Lift it to 90 degrees again with a flexed foot and straight knee.

[8 reps]

Exercise 3

Inhale. Rotate your right leg externally in the hip, straighten your knee, flex the foot, and lift it to the height of the opposite knee.

Exhale. Lower the leg to the height of the opposite ankle. Try to stop the opposite hip from lifting off the floor. Recruit the abdominals and keep the pelvis neutral. If the turnout feels too much of a strain, do the exercise with the leg held parallel to the other.

[4 reps]

Exercise 4

Repeat Exercise 3 but this time with pointed toes on the lifted leg.

[4 reps]

Exercise 5

Prop yourself up on your elbows, your head and shoulders lifted in line with your spine and abdominals scooped.

Inhale. Lift your right leg to the height of the opposite knee with a straight knee and pointed foot.

Exhale. Open your right leg to the side and describe a semicircle in the air with your foot down towards the floor. Keep the pelvis anchored. If you feel the need to lift the opposite hip to the working leg, reduce the circumference of the circles.

Inhale as your leg completes the circle and comes back up.

[4 reps]

Reverse the direction of the circles.

[4 reps]

Exercise 6

Lower yourself back into the supine position.

Inhale. Stretch your right leg along the floor and flex the foot.

Exhale. Throw your right leg up toward your chest. Be careful not to let the buttock lift off the floor.

Inhale. Lower your right leg to the height of the opposite ankle. Control the downward movement – don't let the leg drop.

[8 reps]

Exhale. Relax.

Repeat Exercises 1 to 6 with the other leg.

The Plank

This isometric exercise, as opposed to a contraction and release exercise, helps to strengthen the body in a cross-diagonal way. It challenges the arms, shoulder girdle, and abdominals as well as strengthening the back muscles.

Kneel on all fours and place forearms on the floor with hands clasped. Raise yourself up onto the balls of your feet, and lift the buttocks up towards the ceiling, like a jack-knife. Walk your feet away from your center until your body forms a straight line between shoulders and tailbone. Imagine that you are suspended by a cord leading from your navel to the ceiling.

Hold for as long as you can maintain your form. One minute is a great achievement.

Push-ups

These push-ups further challenge core strength and help control hip extension. They strengthen shoulder muscles and neck flexors, and help achieve coordination of the shoulders and trunk.

Exercise 1

Stand straight with legs and feet parallel, arms by your sides, abdominals engaged.

Inhale.

Exhale. Lower your hands down the front of your legs and place the palms flat on the floor. You will feel a hamstring stretch.

Inhale. Walk your hands away until they are directly under your shoulders.

Exhale. Bring your hips down until they until they are in line with the rest of your body. Make a line from the tip of your head to the back of your heels.

Inhale. Bend your elbows. Try to keep them close to your ribs. Make certain that your abdominals remain engaged. Lower yourself down towards the floor over 6 counts.

Exhale. Push up, straightening your elbows on one count.

[6 reps or more, if you feel you need to increase the challenge]

Exercise 2

Lower yourself into the push-ups position as described above in Exercise 1.

Inhale. Bend your elbows and lower yourself down toward the floor. Engage the abdominals and make certain that your trunk is absolutely stable.

Exhale. Push up, straightening your elbows.

[6 reps]

Stay down on the last push-up with elbows bent and hold for six seconds, breathing normally.

Inhale. Push up and walk hands back to your feet. Try to keep your knees straight and the heels down on the floor.

Exhale. Roll your spine, bone by bone, back into the upright position.

[3 reps or more, if you feel the need to increase the challenge]

Center Work

Your body should now feel thoroughly stretched, stabilized, and responsive, ready to meet the challenge of the center work.

This section is inspired by and modeled on the barre and center work of a classical dance class. The order is progressive from proprioception balancing work, leg work, adagio, petit allegro, to the challenging movement combinations of the cardiovascular section. These combinations will be covered more thoroughly in the Movement Combination section.

Proprioception Exercises

Muscles, tendons, and joints have sensation receptors at the ends of the nerves that activate them. They keep your brain posted as to where your body parts are in relation to each other and in space. You need to continually challenge your proprioceptors so that your body can achieve balance and perfect coordination.

SQUARE DANCING

This exercise involves taking precise steps on the balls of the feet. It helps develop balance and coordination.

Stand straight with legs and feet parallel, arms by your sides. Recruit abdominals, and lift the pelvic floor.

Inhale.

Exhale. Step forward onto the ball of your right foot, a position known as demi-pointe. On a second pulse (short exhalation), join the left foot to the right foot on demi-pointes.

Be careful to take your weight plumb over the ball of the foot onto which you are stepping. Use the body as one unit. Don't drop the back or climb onto the feet by spooning the pelvis.

Inhale. Lower your heels.

Exhale. Step to the right onto the demi-pointe of the right foot, and on the second pulse join the left foot to the right.

Inhale. Lower the heels.

Exhale. Step to the back with the right foot onto the demi-pointe, and on the second pulse, bring the left foot alongside.

Inhale. Lower the heels.

Exhale. Step to the left onto the demi-pointe of the left foot and on the second pulse bring the right foot alongside.

Inhale. Lower your heels to the floor. You have now completed a square.

Repeat the exercise beginning with the left foot.

[4 reps]

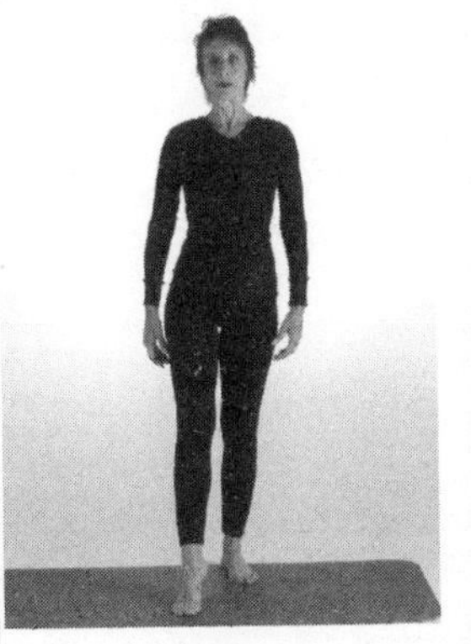

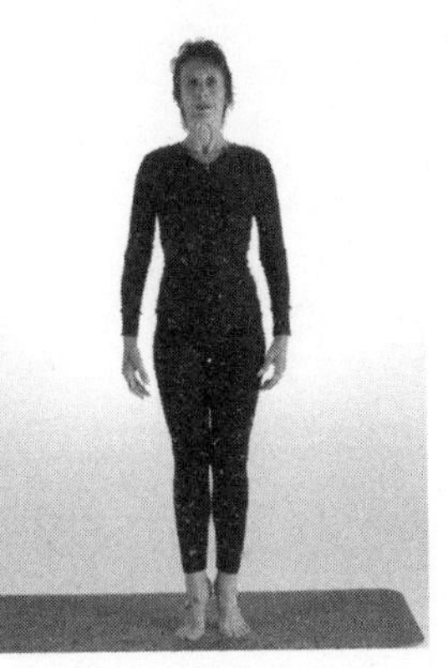

Balancing Exercise

This simple exercise will help to finetune balance.

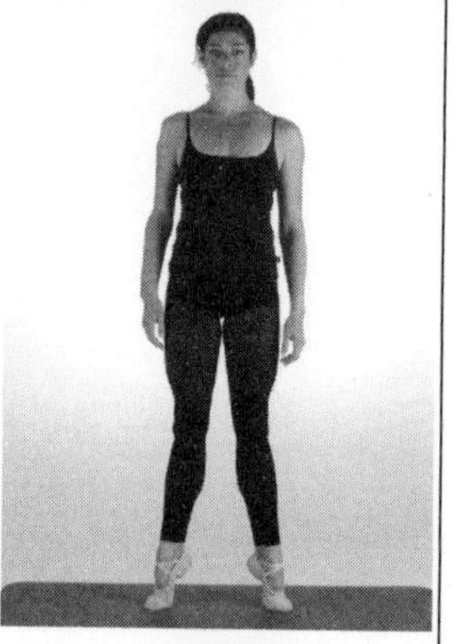

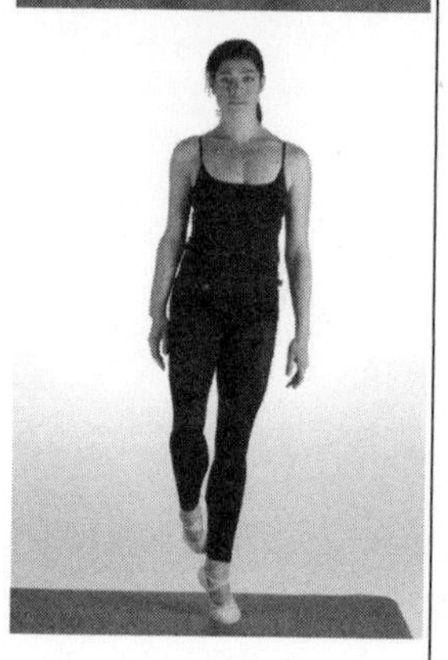

Stand straight with your feet in first position, arms down by your sides. To place yourself in first position, stand with your feet together and pivot on your heels as you rotate the legs laterally at the hip sockets, knees, and feet. Do not force the legs beyond your natural range of flexibility and pay special attention that the turnout at the knees and feet is commensurate with the turnout at the hips.

Squeeze your buttocks and engage your inner thighs. For those people who do not have a great deal of flexibility at the hips, place your feet in a small V.

Inhale. Rise up onto demi-pointe. Bring your shoulders and plumb line over the balls of your feet. Lift your trunk out of the pelvic girdle.

Exhale. Transfer your weight onto the left foot and draw your right foot slowly up the leg to the ankle. You will only need to shift your weight slightly. Do not tilt to the left or settle into the hip. Imagine that the raised foot is lifting up through your mid point in line with the sternum and the crown of your head. Imagine that a ribbon is attached from the top of your head to the ceiling.

Inhale. Return the right foot alongside the left on demi-pointe.

Exhale. Lower your heels.

[8 reps, alternating sides]

When you have mastered the balance with the foot to the ankle, try to lift the foot of the working leg up to the height of the opposite knee.

PLIÉ (KNEE BENDS)

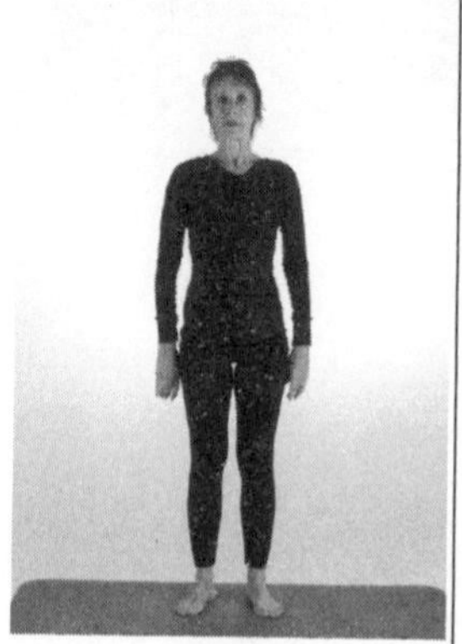

The following exercises will challenge your coordination and balance. This is where Pilates, with its focus on core stability, is an essential tool.

Remember, balance rather than randomness and asymmetry is the secret to moving well. Think carefully about how you organize your body and focus on each and every movement.

Demi-plié

A demi-plié is a small knee bend.

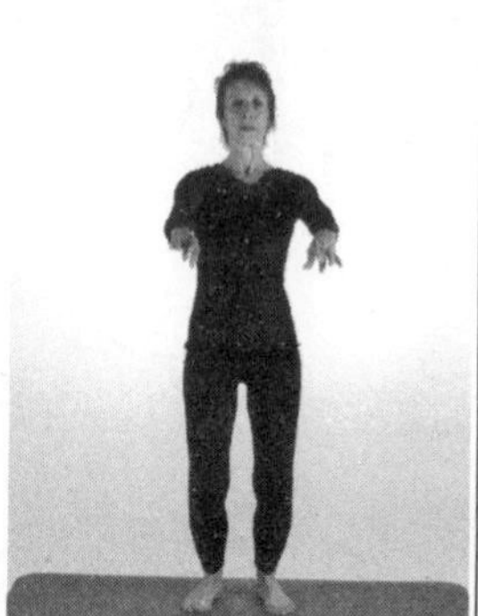

Stand with your feet parallel, hip-width apart, arms down by your sides. Lift out of the waist and recruit your transversus abdominis.

Inhale.

Exhale. Bend at the knees and carefully track them directly over the toes. Take your arms forward to just below shoulder height. Do not roll your feet; the center of gravity should fall between the big and second toes.

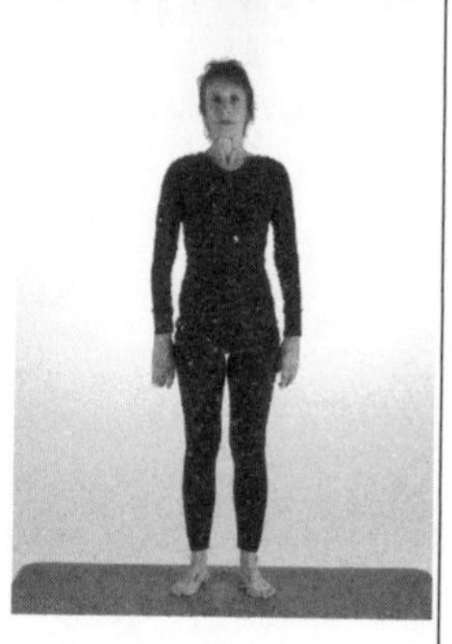

Inhale. Straighten your knees, pulling the patellae directly up toward the pelvis. Do not lock the knees. Lower arms back to the sides.

Exhale.

[8 reps]

Demi-plié with Relevé

This exercise incorporates knee bends with a rise onto the balls of the feet.

Stand with your feet parallel, hip-width apart, arms down by your sides. Lift out of the waist and recruit your transversus abdominis.

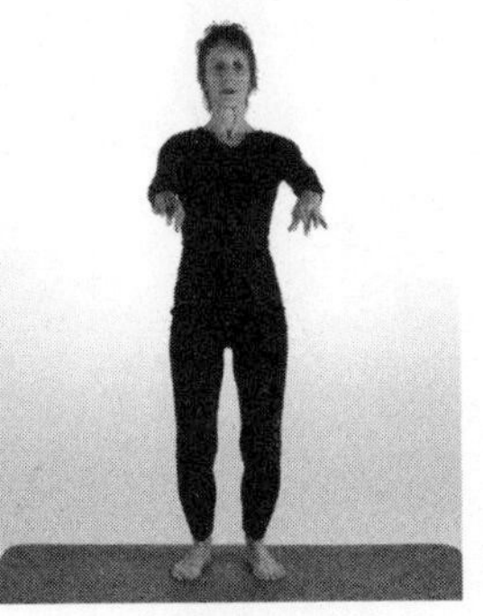

Inhale. Bend your knees directly over the toes. Raise your arms to the front, to just below chest height.

Exhale. Straighten the knees. Bring arms down to the sides.

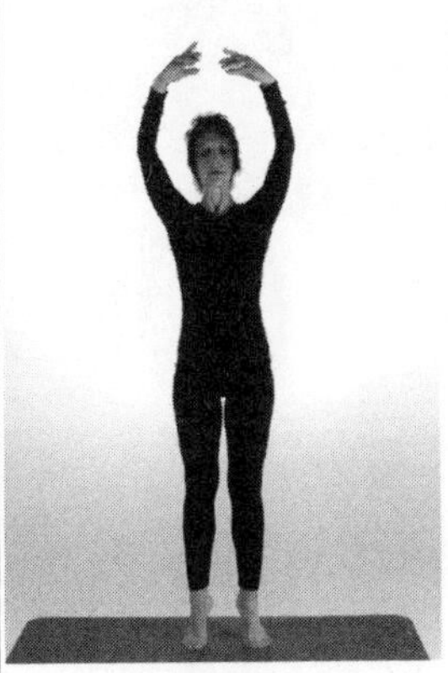

Inhale. Rise up through the feet onto demi-pointe. Take arms forward, palms facing your body, and then lift arms up in front of your head, elbows rounded, palms facing inward. You should be able to see your hands without raising your head.

Exhale. Lower heels. Bring arms down to the sides.

[8 reps]

Demi-plié in First Position

Place yourself in first position – feet forming a V. Hang your arms by your sides, keeping the elbows soft.

Inhale. Bend knees directly over the toes without lifting heels. Lift your arms to the side to reflect the amount of movement at the knees.

Exhale. Pull the knees up straight. Bring the arms down to the sides.

[8 reps]

Demi-plié with Relevé, in First Position

Place yourself in first position, arms relaxed at your sides.

Inhale. Bend knees directly over toes without lifting heels. Raise arms to the sides, to about 45 degrees.

Exhale. Straighten the knees and lower your arms to your sides.

Inhale. Roll through the feet onto demi-pointe. Take arms forward, palms facing your body, and then lift arms up, in front of your head, elbows rounded, palms facing inward. You should be able to see your hands without moving your head up.

Exhale. Lower your heels to the floor, keeping the knees straight. Open your arms to the sides and bring them down beside your body.

[8 reps]

Full Plié

A full plié, or deep knee bend, looks easy but isn't. This is an advanced exercise – it will really challenge the strength and control in your entire body.

It will mobilize and strengthen the knees, leg adductors, glutei, and trunk stabilisers, as well as stretch the Achilles tendon.

Stand with your feet in first position, knees straight, arms relaxed by your sides.

Inhale. Take your arms forward to just below chest height, slightly rounded at the elbows.

Exhale. Open your arms to the side with soft elbows.

Inhale. Bend your knees directly over your toes, keeping the heels pressed into the floor. Feel the stretch at the Achilles tendon. Lower your arms to the sides of your body.

Exhale. Continue to push down until the heels need to lift slightly off the floor. Press the knees back. Lift the arms forward, to just below the chest.

Inhale. Begin to ascend. Lower the heels to the floor as soon as possible. Keep the back straight and don't spoon at the pelvis or drop the shoulders.

Exhale. Straighten the knees by pulling the patellae up toward the pelvis. Open your arms to the side.

[8 reps]

Full Plié with Relevé

Execute a full plié, as described above.

Inhale. Roll through the feet and rise up onto demi-pointe. At the same time, take your arms forward with rounded elbows and lift them up in front of your head. Keep the palms in range of vision.

Exhale. Lower the heels down to the floor and open the arms back out to the side.

[4 reps]

Full Plié in Second Position

Perform the following two exercises seamlessly.

Exercise 1

Stand in second position, arms relaxed by your sides. To place yourself in second position, stand with your feet slightly wider than hip-width apart. Rotate on your heels so that your toes point outward in a comfortable V.

Inhale. Lift your arms to the front, just below chest height, palms facing your body, elbows softly rounded.

Exhale. Open your arms to the side, elbows soft.

Inhale. Bend your knees directly over the toes. Count 1. Engage the inside thigh muscles (adductors) to hold the knees open. The glutei should assist in

holding the turnout by wrapping around the tops of the legs like cabbage leaves. Do not tense the buttocks. At the same time, lower your arms down to your sides.

Exhale. Continue to bend the knees out to the side without lifting the heels. Count 2 at this point.

Inhale. Begin the ascent, keeping the back straight and the knees pressed open. Pull the patellae directly up the legs toward the hip bones. At the same time, raise the softly rounded arms to the front, to just below the chest. Count 3.

Exhale. Finish with the knees straight and arms open to the side. Count 4.

[8 reps]

Exercise 2

This really works the glutei and thigh muscles.

Repeat the full pliés in second position but in two counts. Hold the arms to the side at shoulder height.

Inhale. Pull up out of the hips.

Exhale. Bend the knees to the side over the toes. Count 1 as you finish this movement.

Inhale. Pull the knees up straight. Count 2.

[16 reps]

Port de Bras à la Seconde

Port de bras means "carriage of the arms". Here it is performed with side bends. Try not to think of this as purely an exercise but instead let yourself feel the quality of the movement. Open up your body, and express yourself. Link one movement with the next, maintaining a steady flow of energy.

Stand with your feet parallel, arms down by your sides.

Inhale. Lift your arms forward to just below chest height, slightly rounded at the elbows.

Exhale. Open your arms to the side with soft elbows.

Inhale. Step to the side onto your right foot. Place your left foot beside the right. Bend your knees as you lift your right arm overhead.

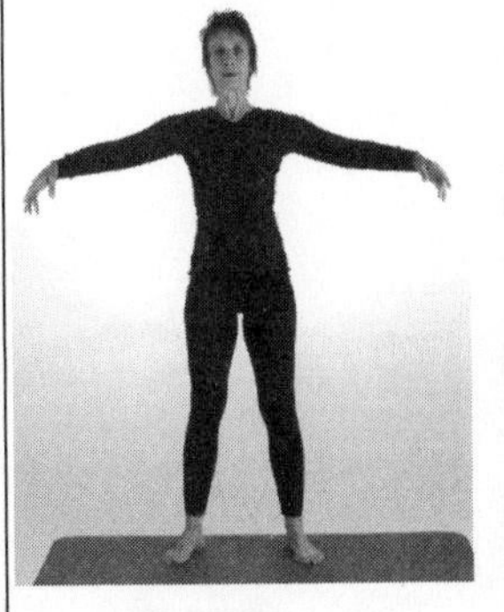

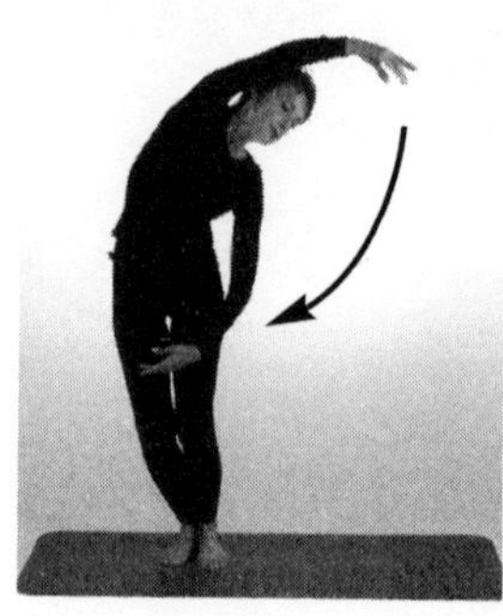

Exhale. Lengthen though your spine and bend from the waist to the left wall. Imagine that you are trying to touch the opposite wall with your fingers. Your upper body should be parallel to the floor. Do not dive down towards the floor and crunch your ribs.

Continue to circle the right arm down in front of your body and finish with it open to the side. Follow the path of your hand with your gaze, gently rolling the head, so that you are looking to the right at the finish. Feel the stretch across your shoulder blades and expand your chest.

Inhale. Straighten the knees and step to the left with the left foot. Close your right foot beside it. Bend your knees and lift your left arm up toward the ceiling. Pull up out of the pelvis.

Exhale. Bend your upper body to the right and try to touch the right wall. Keep circling the left arm in front of the body and finish with it open to the side and with the head turned to the left.

Inhale. Straighten your knees and step to the right, and so on.

[8 reps]

Battement Tendu en Croix

This exercise isolates movement in the hip joint and strengthens the iliopsoas – when you stand on one leg with the trunk positioned over the hip and aligned with the foot, the iliopsoas is central to achieving balance. The exercise involves leg extensions performed in a cross shape, and as well as exercising the muscles in the legs and feet, it is designed to integrate muscle groups.

Keep your trunk square and stabilized while you are working your legs in different directions. Don't lose the neutral position of the hips.

Stand in first position. Only turn out as much as you can without feeling stress on the knees.

Inhale. Lift arms forward to just below chest height, slightly rounded at the elbows.

Exhale. Open arms to the side with soft elbows.

Inhale. Lengthen the spine and lift up out of the pelvic girdle.

Exhale. Brush your right foot forward along the floor, leading with the heel – transfer your weight onto the left leg, though it will only be a subtle shift – and keeping hips neutral. As soon as possible, lift your right heel and point your foot, keeping your leg and foot turned out.

Inhale. Flex your right foot and draw it back to the first position by brushing the whole foot along the floor.

Exhale. Shift the weight back onto two feet as you close the right foot into first position. Arms should remain open at your sides.

[4 reps]

Continue seamlessly into battement tendu to the side.

Inhale. Pull up out of the hips, lengthen the spine, recruit abdominals.

Exhale. Transfer weight onto your left leg. Slide right foot along the floor to the side. Point the foot. There should be no weight on the pointed foot.

Inhale. Flex foot and draw it back along the floor.

Exhale. Shift the weight back onto two feet as you close the right foot into first position.

[4 reps]

Continue seamlessly into battement tendu to the back. The leg extensions to the back are the most difficult. Not only are you required to keep the working leg turned out, but you also need to keep the hip bones aligned and the back supported.

Inhale. Pull up out of the hips, lengthen the spine, recruit abdominals.

Exhale. Slide the right foot along the floor, lift the heel and point your foot.

Transfer your weight onto the left leg, shift the shoulders slightly forward and square the hips.

Inhale. Flex foot and slide it back into first position.

Exhale.

[4 reps]

Continue seamlessly into another set of four battement tendus to the side, leading with the right foot.

Repeat the sequence above, with 4 reps each to the side, front, back, and then side again.

Exhale. Relax and prepare to repeat the whole combination, this time leading with the left foot.

[2 reps]

Dégagé en Croix

This exercise is made up of leg extensions at a 45-degree angle, in the shape of a cross.

To place yourself in third position, place the right heel against the inside middle of your left foot and rotate both legs outwards – at the hips, knees, and feet. Squeeze the buttocks and the backs of the upper inner thighs together.

Inhale. Lift arms forward to just below chest height, slightly rounded at the elbows.

Exhale. Open arms to the sides with soft elbows.

Inhale. Slide the right foot forward, leading with the heel. Lift the heel and point the foot, and then lift the leg to a 45-degree angle.

Exhale. Flex foot, lower it to the floor and pull it back to third position, deliberately engaging the inner thigh muscle (adductors). Imagine that you are listening to music and that you are bringing the foot back to third position on each beat.

[8 reps]

Continue seamlessly into dégagé to the side.

Inhale. Slide the right foot along the floor to the side, leading with the heel. Point the foot and raise the leg to 45 degrees.

Exhale. Flex foot and close the right foot to the back of the left foot on the first dégagé.

On the second dégagé, close the heel of the right foot to the front of the left foot.

[8 reps]

Continue seamlessly into dégagé to the back.

Inhale. Slide the foot along the floor to the back, directly in line with your hip. Maintain the turnout and keep your trunk square. Point the foot and raise the leg to 45 degrees behind you.

Exhale. Flex foot and close the right foot back into third position.

[8 reps]

Continue seamlessly into 8 more reps of dégagés to the side with the right leg.

[4 reps]

Repeat the combination with the left leg.

[4 reps]

Knee Lifts

The following exercises strengthen the quads and core muscles of the torso, and balance the iliopsoas and all the surrounding structures of the pelvis.

Stand with your feet parallel, hip-width apart.

Inhale. Take your arms forward to just below chest height, slightly rounded at the elbows.

Exhale. Open your arms to the side with soft elbows.

Inhale.

Exhale. Lift your thigh up towards your chest. Be careful to hold your back upright throughout the exercise.

Inhale. Place the foot back on to the floor – toe, ball, heel.

Exhale.

[16 reps, alternating legs]

Knee Lifts with Knee Bends

Stand with your feet parallel, hip-width apart.

Inhale. Take your arms forward to just below chest height, slightly rounded at the elbows.

Exhale. Open your arms to the side with soft elbows.

Inhale. Bend both knees directly over your feet.

Exhale. Lift your right knee towards your chest, straightening the other leg at the same time.

Inhale. Place the raised foot down on the floor and bend your knees.

Exhale. Relax.

[16 reps, alternating legs]

Knee Lifts with Knee Bends in Second Position

Place your feet in second position.

Inhale. Take your arms forward to just below chest height, slightly rounded at the elbows.

Exhale. Open your arms to the side with soft elbows.

Inhale. Bend both knees directly over your feet.

Exhale. Lift your right knee up to the side, keeping it turned out at the hip. Straighten the other leg at the same time.

Inhale. Place the raised foot down on the floor and bend your knees.

Exhale. Relax.

[16 reps, alternating legs]

Retiré

This is a move where one pointed foot is lifted and placed against the opposite knee. It improves proprioception, stabilizes and strengthens the pelvic girdle, and improves muscle coordination in the lower limbs. The retiré also develops the alignment of spine and trunk.

Stand with your feet in first position, arms down by your sides. Lift your body out of the pelvic girdle and center your weight.

Inhale. Lift arms forward to just below chest height, with slightly rounded elbows.

Exhale. Open arms to the side with soft elbows.

Inhale. Point your toes and lift your right foot to the front of the left ankle. Keep your thigh open and knee pressed to the side.

Exhale. Draw your foot higher up the leg to the side of the opposite knee.

Inhale. Change your foot to the back of the leg and lower it to the back of the left ankle.

Exhale. Lift the right leg back to the side of the left knee.

Inhale. Slide it back down the leg to the front of the left ankle.

Exhale. Close the right foot back into first position. Keep your arms out to the side.

[8 reps, alternating legs]

Fondu in Attitude

This is a position in which one leg is extended off the floor with a bent knee. It improves balance, coordination of lower limbs, and strengthens core muscles.

Stand with your feet in first position.

Inhale. Lift your arms to the front just below chest height, slightly rounded at the elbows.

Exhale. Open your arms to the side with soft elbows.

Inhale. Bend both knees and lift the right foot to the front of the left ankle. Keep your right knee in a turned out position.

Exhale. Open your right leg to the front, leading with the heel, knee still bent and turned out at an angle of more than 90 degrees.

Inhale. Rotate your right leg at the hip joint towards the left leg until it is parallel with it, keeping the knee at the same angle. The opposite knee is still bent.

Exhale. Turn the right leg out.

Inhale. Turn the right leg back in to parallel and so on.

[4 reps]

Inhale. Return your right foot back to the left ankle.

Exhale. Straighten both knees and return your right foot to first position.

Repeat with the left leg.

Then repeat both legs once more.

Exhale. Straighten both knees and lower the arms down beside the body.

Fondu en Croix

To improve balance, coordination of lower limbs, and strengthen core muscles.

Stand with your feet in first position.

Inhale. Lift arms forward to just below chest height, slightly rounded at the elbows.

Exhale. Open your arms to the side with soft elbows.

Inhale. Bend both knees and bring your right foot, toes pointed, to the front of the left ankle.

Exhale. Straighten both legs with the right leg stretched at an angle of 45 degrees to the front.

Inhale. Bring your right foot back to the left ankle while simultaneously bending the left knee. Remember to hold your thighs and knees open to the side like a window.

Exhale. Straighten both legs, this time opening the right leg out to the side at 45 degrees (dégagé).

Inhale. Place your right foot to the back of the left ankle while bending the left knee.

Exhale. Stretch both legs but this time straighten the right leg to the back. Keep your hipbones aligned and the right leg turned out.

Inhale. Return your foot to the back of the right ankle while bending your left knee at the same time.

Exhale. Straighten both legs opening the right leg to the side.

Inhale. Bend both knees and return the right foot to the front of the left ankle.

Exhale.

You've now completed one repetition of "fondu en croix" – to the front, side, back, and side.

[4 reps]

Inhale. Place your foot back into first position.

Exhale. Straighten your knees and bring your arms back down to your sides.

Swap legs.

[4 reps]

When you have mastered this exercise you can attempt to do it with a relevé. To add this to the exercise, continue to roll through the supporting foot up onto demi-pointe when you have straightened both legs. Then, as you bend the knees and bring the working foot back to the opposite ankle, roll back down through the foot.

As you get stronger try to lift the working leg to an extension of 90 degrees, but don't sacrifice form for height. Keep the correct placement, particularly at the hips and shoulders. Don't sit into the hips. When you arrive in extension, make certain that both knees are fully pulled up.

Rond de Jambe

Rond de jambe, *which means "round of the leg", refers to a half circle drawn with the foot. It promotes mobility in the hip joint, pelvic stability, and coordination of the lower limbs.*

Stand in first position, arms down by your sides.

Inhale. Lift arms forward to just below chest height, slightly rounded at the elbows.

Exhale. Open arms to the side with soft elbows.

Inhale. Slide your right foot forward leading with the heel until the foot points. Trace a circle with your foot and leg to the side and around to the back.

Exhale. Lower your right heel and bring the foot forward. Pass it through first position with the foot flat on the floor. Be careful not to roll the foot.

[8 reps]

Inhale. Place your feet back in first position.

Exhale.

Reverse the cycle.

Inhale. Begin by pointing the foot to the back. Circle to the side, then to the front.

Exhale. Lower the heel to the floor and draw the foot backwards. Pass the foot through first position to the back, in line with the right shoulder.

[8 reps]

Exhale. Close your foot to first position and lower your arms to your sides.

Repeat with the other leg.

Modified Arabesque

To develop strength in your back, shoulders, abdominals, and the lower limbs.

This is a position where one leg is lifted behind the body.

Stand with your legs and feet together in parallel, arms by your sides.

Inhale. Slide your right foot to the back until it points. Keep your hips and shoulders square. Press the palms of your hands together in front of your sternum.

Exhale. Lift your right leg off the floor and extend your upper body forward, in line with the leg. Use your hands as a sight line down the center as you straighten the elbows and reach away with the fingertips. Recruit your abdominals. Imagine that you are suspended by a cord leading from your belly button to the ceiling. Your head and neck are aligned with your spine. Aim for one straight line from the fingertips to the toes of the extended leg.

Hold for 30 seconds.

Remember to keep the spine supported by the abdominals for the duration of the pose.

Swap legs.

[2 reps]

Adagio (Slow, Controlled Movements)

Most dancers have a love-hate relationship with adagio combinations. This is because while the movements should look effortless, seamless, and graceful, they know that this appearance belies the intense effort involved in their performance.

Slow, deliberate exercises require precise placement, balance, and strength. This takes time and patience to achieve but the end result is rewarding.

Plié, Port de Bras & Temps Lié

This exercise consists of knee bends, an upper body stretch to the side, and weight transferal.

Stand with your feet in a wide second position. Lengthen through the spine, lift the pelvic floor, and pull up out of the waist. Recruit the abdominals.

Inhale. Take your arms forward to just below chest height, slightly rounded at the elbows.

Exhale. Open arms to the side with soft elbows.

Inhale. Bend your knees directly over the feet.

Exhale. Transfer your weight onto the right leg and lunge to the side. Straighten the left leg and point your toes. Do not put any weight on the left foot. Raise the left arm overhead. Bend to the right side at the waist, upper body parallel to the floor, both arms reaching towards the right wall.

Inhale. Circle the left arm down past the front of the body and transfer your weight back to the center, bending your knees as you open your left arm back to the side. Gently roll your head, following the path of your arm with your eyes.

Exhale. Straighten the knees and pull up through the middle.

Inhale. Bend your knees directly over the feet.

Exhale. Transfer the weight onto the left leg and lunge to the side. Straighten the right leg and point your toes. Raise the right arm overhead. Bend to the left side at the waist, both arms reaching towards the left wall.

Inhale. Circle the right arm down past the front of the body and transfer your weight back to the center, bending your knees as you open your right arm back to the side. Gently roll your head, following the path of your arm with your eyes.

Exhale. Straighten the knees and pull up through the middle.

[8 reps]

Plié, Port de Bras, Temps Lié & Arabesque

This exercise includes a knee bend, an upper body stretch, weight transferal and a balance.

Stand with your feet in a wide second position. Lengthen through the spine, lift the pelvic floor, and pull up out of the waist. Recruit the abdominals.

Inhale. Take your arms forward to just below chest height, slightly rounded at the elbows.

Exhale. Open arms to the side with soft elbows.

Inhale. Bend knees directly over toes.

Exhale. Transfer your weight onto the right leg and lunge to the side. Straighten the left leg and point your toes. Do not have any weight on the pointed foot. Lift the left arm overhead.

Bend to the right side at the waist, upper body parallel to the floor, stretching both arms toward the right wall.

Pivot on the right foot to face the right wall. Your left leg is now directly in line with your left shoulder and your trunk and shoulders are parallel to the floor.

Inhale. Lift your left leg off the floor in line with your spine and head.

Exhale. Place the left foot back onto the floor.

Inhale. Pivot on the right foot and return to face the front, still bending at the waist with the upper body parallel to the floor and the arms reaching toward the right wall.

Exhale.

Inhale. Circle the left arm down past the front of your body and transfer your weight back to your center, bending your knees. Open your left arm back to the side. Gently roll your head while following the path of your arm with your eyes.

Exhale. Straighten your knees and pull up though the middle.

Swap sides.

[8 reps]

Posé Arabesque

This exercise requires a great deal of strength and control as well as good proprioception. It involves stepping onto one leg and lifting the other leg behind you.

Stand straight with your feet in first position.

Inhale. Raise your arms to the front of your body just below the chest.

Exhale. Open your arms to the side with soft elbows.

Inhale. Slide your right foot forward along the floor and point it, lifting it off the floor to a 45-degree angle. At the same time, bend your left knee. Imagine that you are taking a wide step over a swollen creek, from one bank to the other.

Exhale. Step onto the right foot – toe, ball, heel – and bend your right knee to cushion your landing.

Inhale. Lift and extend your left leg behind you with a straight knee. Don't let it hang like a dog's hind leg.

Make certain that your weight is well over your supporting leg and that your knee is directly over your toes. Do not drop your back. Engage your abdominals and stabilize your shoulder blades.

Exhale. Pull up and stretch your right knee. Straighten your body. Pass the heel of the left foot by the heel of the right and extend it to the front, lifting it to 45 degrees. At the same time bend the right knee.

Inhale to prepare.

Exhale. Step onto the left foot. Remember to step beyond your toes, more of a stride than a cautious step. Bend the left knee as you land and extend the right leg out to the back.

[4 reps]

Then reverse the exercise. Begin by sliding the right foot to the back. You will be stepping over the creek backwards.

Try not to tilt your trunk backwards when you land on your foot. Your shoulders should be directly over your supporting foot.

[4 reps]

When you have mastered stepping over the creek, try to spring across. The mechanics remain the same. Always bend the knee and push down into the heel before you jump.

Grand Battement en Cloche

This exercise combines strength, flexibility, and coordination – the leg is swung like a bell.

Stand with your feet in first position.

Inhale. Lift your arms to the front just below chest height, slightly rounded at the elbows.

Exhale. Open arms to the side with soft elbows.

Inhale. Pull your patellae up and lift out of the hips. Recruit the abdominals. Slide your right foot along the floor to the back in line with your right shoulder. Lift the heel and point the foot.

Exhale. Lower your heel, slide your right foot flat along the floor past the left heel and kick your leg up to the front with a bent knee angled at more than 90 degrees.

Inhale. Lower the right foot to the floor. Pass it through first position up into a kick to the back with a bent knee, angled at slightly more than 90 degrees. The leg should be turned out in the hip.

Let the trunk and shoulders adjust slightly forward as the leg swings to the back, but do not drop your spine or release the abdominals. Control the descent of your leg, resisting gravity as your foot floats back to first position.

The supporting leg should be pulled up throughout.

[8 reps]

Inhale. Close the leg into the first position.

Exhale. Lower the arms back down to your sides.

Swap legs.

[8 reps]

The exercise above can be done with a straight working leg, but only if you have enough hamstring flexibility and enough control. If you find yourself wobbling, be patient and try it again at a later date when you have developed more strength.

Grand Rond de Jambe en l'Air

In this exercise you will draw large circles in the air with the leg. This will mobilize hip rotators, and challenge and strengthen the core stabilizing muscles.

Stand with your feet in first position.

Inhale. Lift arms to the front of your body, just below chest height, slightly rounded at the elbows.

Exhale. Open your arms to the side with soft elbows.

Inhale. Leading with the heel, slide the right foot to the front along the floor.

Exhale. Lift your leg, maintaining the turnout in the hip, and angle your knee to just a little more than 90 degrees. Keep your heel raised as if you want to balance a teacup on it.

Inhale. Hold leg in the turned-out raised position.

Exhale. Rotate the leg open to the side, leading with the knee. Be careful not to let the leg dip down. The knee should circle the entire circumference at the same level. Keep pulling up on the supporting leg. Lift the trunk out of the pelvic girdle.

Inhale. Hold.

Exhale. Leading with the knee, rotate leg to the back. Maintain the turnout. Take your shoulders slightly forward to accommodate the leg at the back. Ideally the thigh should be parallel to the floor.

Inhale. Hold.

Exhale. Straighten the leg into an arabesque. Do not lean forward.

Inhale. Lower the pointed foot to the floor.

Exhale. Close the foot into the first position and lower your arms down to your sides.

Change legs.

[4 reps each side]

Brain Teaser

Aim to move seamlessly from one exercise to the next in this set of exercises. This sequence is trickier than it appears – you'll find that you have to concentrate hard throughout. It challenges proprioception, flexibility and strength.

Exercise 1

Stand with your legs turned out in a wide second position (about one and a half of your own feet wide). Remember not to force the rotation. Hold your arms open to the side.

Inhale. Bend the knees.

Exhale. Transfer your weight onto the left leg, straighten the knee and extend your right leg out to the side, just above the floor at 45 degrees.

Inhale. Bring the right foot back to meet the left, so that your weight is in the center. Bend your knees.

Exhale. Transfer your weight onto the right leg and extend the left leg out to the side at 45 degrees. Don't tilt your body from side to side, the weight shift is only minimal.

[10 reps]

Exercise 2

Repeat the above but this time when you move the leg out to the side, lift it as high as you can with a bent knee.

The knee should be directed towards the armpit.

[10 reps]

Exercise 3

Once again, stand with your legs turned out in a wide second position. Hold your arms open to the side.

Inhale. Then bend your knees with your weight in the middle.

Exhale. Transfer your weight onto the left leg, straighten the left knee, and extend your right leg out to the side with a high bent knee, as in Exercise 2.

Draw the right knee across the body, medially rotating the leg, and simultaneously swing both arms across the body in the opposite direction. Turn your head in the same direction as your hands.

Inhale. Return your weight back to the center with bent knees, arms open to the sides.

Exhale. Transfer your weight onto the right leg and extend the left leg out to the side. Extend your left leg out to the side with a high bent knee. Draw the left knee across the body, simultaneously swinging both arms across to the right, followed by the head.

[10 reps]

Repeat Exercises 1 to 3.

[4 reps]

Petit Allegro (Small Jumps)

As in the rest of the workout, this section requires focus and attention to correct placement as well as plenty of practice. The quality of a jump depends on several factors: the strength of the leg muscles; the elasticity and strength of the ligaments of the foot and knee; a well-developed Achilles tendon; the strength of the toes, and especially the strength of the thighs.

Always prepare for a jump with a demi-plié (knee bends with the heels pressed into the floor). Never lift the heel during the push off. The more you press into the floor with the whole foot before take off, the higher you will jump. At the high point of the jump, the knees, insteps, and toes must be fully stretched. The landing must always be soft. At first, the toes touch the floor then the weight is taken through the foot onto the sole. The knees bend to cushion the impact.

Jumping can be exhilarating. Experience the thrill of momentary weightlessness.

IMPORTANT

Never perform jumps on concrete – make sure it is a wooden floor.

SAUTÉ

A sauté is a small jump from two feet back onto two feet. It coordinates preparation, take-off and suspension, three requirements for the development of ballon (the ability to pause in midair).

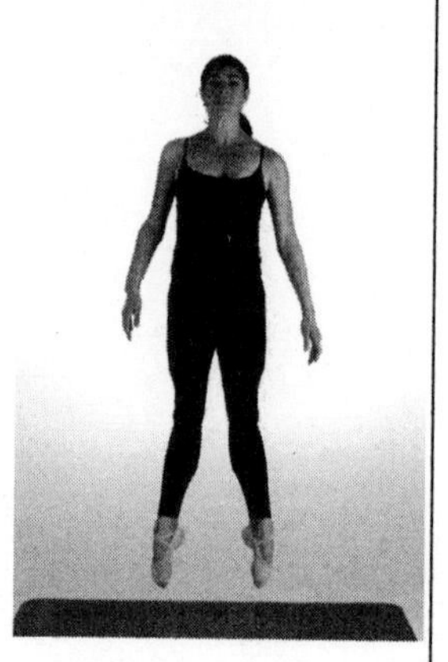

Stand straight with your feet in first position, arms down by your sides.

Inhale. Bend your knees directly over your toes, press down through your feet and jump. Stretch your knees and point your toes. Use your leg muscles. Don't strain with your neck and shoulders, and don't spoon the pelvis.

Exhale. Land back on the floor, working through your feet – toe, ball, heel – and bend your knees. Keep your back straight.

[8 reps, with the accent on the landing]

Repeat, but this time place the accent on the jump. This means that you prepare on the inhalation, and jump on the exhalation. Try to pause in midair.

[8 reps]

Sauté en Tournant

This exercise combines a simple jump on the spot with moving around in a circle. Remember to breathe evenly and deeply throughout the exercise. Watch against breathing shallowly as you tire.

Stand straight with your feet in first position, arms down by your sides.

Execute 4 sautés facing the front.

Then execute 4 sautés, turning by quarters, clockwise. Your first jump will land at three o'clock, the second at 6 o'clock facing the back wall, the third to the left wall at 9 o'clock and the fourth will land so that you are facing the front.

Repeat 4 sautés en place and four sautés en tournant, but this time circle anti-clockwise.

[4 reps in each direction]

Sauté & Echappé

Stand straight with your feet in first position, arms down by your sides.

Do 4 sautés en place, counting 1, 2, 3, 4.

Now begin the echappés.

Jump and land with your feet apart in second position when you count 1.

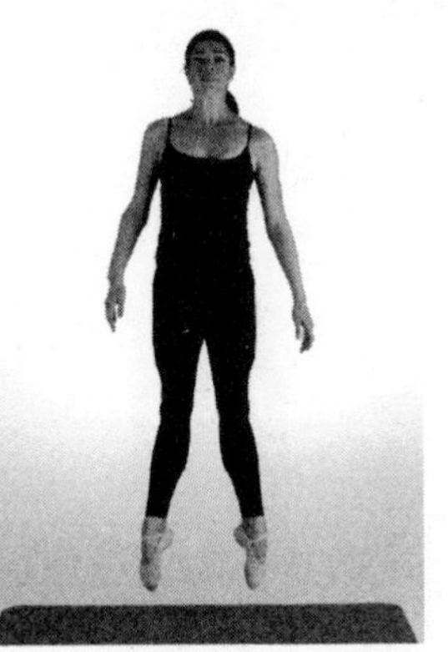

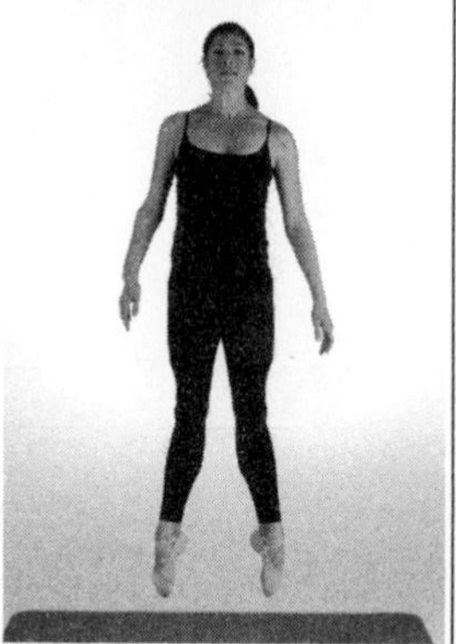

Jump and bring your feet back to the first position when you count 2.

Jump out to second position again, on count 3.

And jump back to first position on count 4.

Accompany yourself by singing along, 1, 2, 3, 4, out, in, out, in and so on.

[16 reps]

Sauté & Petit Jeté

These exercises incorporate a small jump from one foot to the other.

Exercise 1

Stand straight with your feet in first position, arms down by your sides.

Execute 8 sautés. Jump off both feet and land on both feet.

Execute 8 jetés. Jump off two feet and land with the left toes at the back of the right ankle at the back of the right ankle, right knee bent.

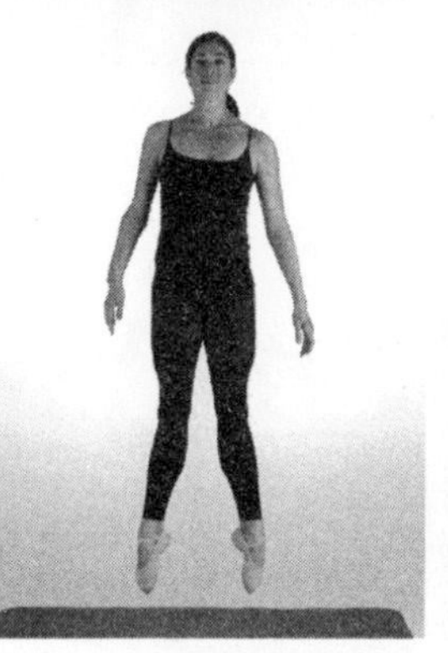

Jump off the right foot and land on the left with the right foot lifted to the back of the left ankle, left knee bent.

[Alternate sides for 8 reps]

Then execute 8 sautés – jumping off both feet and landing on both feet.

Now perform 8 jetés – jump off two feet and land on the right foot with the left foot at the front of the right ankle.

Jump off the right foot and land on the left with the right foot at the front of the left ankle, alternating 8 times.

Exercise 2

Now repeat Exercise 1 but with the leg lifted to attitude. This means that the knee will be angled at just more than 90 degrees in the jetés.

Execute 8 sautés.

Execute 8 jetés – jump off two feet and land on the right foot with the knee bent. Lift the left leg to the front with the knee angled at just more than 90 degrees, keeping the leg turned out at the hip.

Jump off right foot and land on the left, lift the right leg to the front.

[8 reps, alternating legs]

Execute 8 sautés.

Execute 8 jetés. Jump off two feet and land on the right foot, knee bent. Lift the left leg to the back. Try to keep it turned out and the angle at the knee at more than 90 degrees.

Jump onto the left foot and raise the right leg to the back.

[8 reps, alternating sides]

Movement Combinations

Any seasoned dancer will tell you that knowing how to pace yourself is essential if you want to make it through a four act ballet. So take a breather because now that you have mastered some of the nitty gritty, let's get a little more energetic and challenge your muscular endurance and cardiorespiratory system.

To achieve aerobic fitness, the resting heart rate must be lowered. For any activity to be aerobically effective, try for a target rate of between 55 percent and 90 percent of your maximum heart rate, which is 220 beats a minute minus your age. Your ideal heart rate should be 55–90 percent of that maximum rate. Once you have learnt some of the following combinations try to do them seamlessly for 10 to 20 minutes.

It is recommended you have a medical check up before you do any type of aerobic exercise.

In this section, remember to control your breathing – keep it even, rhythmic, and let it flow with your movements.

Chassé (Chased)

This is the dancer's version of a gallop. You can do them in any direction. Chassés are used for linking steps or on their own. Once you have mastered the mechanics, have some fun with this combination. It feels great when you do a number of chassés in succession.

Exercise 1

Stand up straight with your feet in first position, arms relaxed by your sides.

Bend both knees to the side without lifting the heels off the floor.

Slide your right foot along the floor to the side. As you bring your left foot in to meet the right, push off the floor from both feet and lift yourself slightly into the air.

Join your feet together in the air and point them. Imagine you are galloping to the side, without lifting your legs too high, so that one leg chases the other.

Control your breathing and remember never to hold your breath.

[8 reps, in alternating directions]

Exercise 2

Now add in the arm movements.

Slide your right foot to the side and swing both arms in front of your body to the right. Circle them overhead as you bring your feet together.

Execute 4 chassés to the right, circling the arms anticlockwise, followed by 4 chassés to the left, circling the arms clockwise.

[8 reps]

Dance Sequence I

Now we are going to challenge your memory by combining a few steps into a short dance sequence. This is the time to bring some panache into the action. Remember the entire body participates to create beautiful posture while standing still or in action. It's all about the concept of line, from your head to your toes, from your pointed foot to leg to torso to arm to hand. Even your eyes can help. Where your eyes go, your body follows. So level your eyes at your imaginary audience, feel good about yourself, and dance!

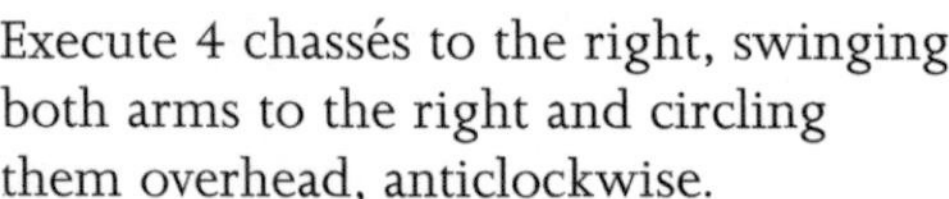

Execute 4 chassés to the right, swinging both arms to the right and circling them overhead, anticlockwise.

Execute 4 chassés to the left, swinging both arms to the left and circling them overhead, clockwise.

Execute 1 chassé to the right circling both arms anticlockwise. Step on the right foot, bend the knee, and jump, lifting the left foot up to the opposite knee, with the left knee parallel to the right. Lift the right arm up towards the ceiling and hold the left arm out to the side.

Execute 1 chassé to the left, swinging arms clockwise. Step onto the left foot, bend the knee, and jump. This time lift the right foot up to the side of the left knee and lift your left arm up towards the ceiling and hold your right arm out to the side.

Repeat the sequence above, moving clockwise in a small circle. Repeat the sequence until you are facing the front again.

Then begin the whole sequence again, this time starting with the left foot. This time circle anticlockwise.

[4 reps or more]

BALANCÉ (WALTZ STEP)

This is another opportunity to release the dancer in you. Feel the flow, enjoy the expansive movements and use the full amount of space available. If you haven't got a Strauss disc on hand, hum a waltz tempo to yourself: 1, 2, 3, 1, 2, 3, and so on. Keep the tempo steady.

Exercise 1

Stand with your feet in first position.

Exhale. Open your arms to the side and place your hands on your hips.

Count 1. Step onto your right foot, raise your left foot off the floor and place pointed toes to the back of the right ankle.

Count 2. Step down. Put your weight onto the ball of the left foot, lifting the right foot off the floor.

Count 3. Lower your right foot back to the floor, bend your knee, and place all your weight over that leg. Lift your left foot to the right ankle.

Hum: Step, lift, down, step, lift, down, and so on.

[16 reps]

Exercise 2

Now add in some arm movements.

Stand in first position.

Take your arms forward and the open them to the side. As you step to the right, swing the left arm across your body, to the right, lifting the right arm at the same time.

As you step to the left, swing both arms across the body to the left.

Go for 16 reps covering the floor space with expansive steps, moving from side to side.

Exercise 3

You can also perform balancés traveling forwards and backwards.

Just step the back foot a little further away from the front, if you are traveling backwards. If you are traveling forwards, place the second foot to the front of the first.

Try 8 reps of each to practice.

Then perform:

- 4 balancés forward
- 4 balancés backward
- 4 balancés traveling around in a small circle, clockwise until you are back facing the front
- 4 balancés moving from side to side, stepping out with the right foot and placing the left foot behind it.

Repeat the above.

Then begin with the left foot, and execute 4 balancés traveling forward.

Then begin with the right foot, and execute 4 balancés traveling backward.

Follow this with 4 balancés circling anticlockwise, then four balancés from side to side.

[Repeat, alternating sides]

Traveling Lunges

This exercise is loosely based on posé tombé. It exercises the glutei as well as the leg muscles, especially the quadriceps. If you haven't got enough traveling space in your living room, you can do these up and down your hallway.

Stand with your feet parallel, hip-width apart, arms down by your sides.

Step forward onto the demi-pointe of your right foot.

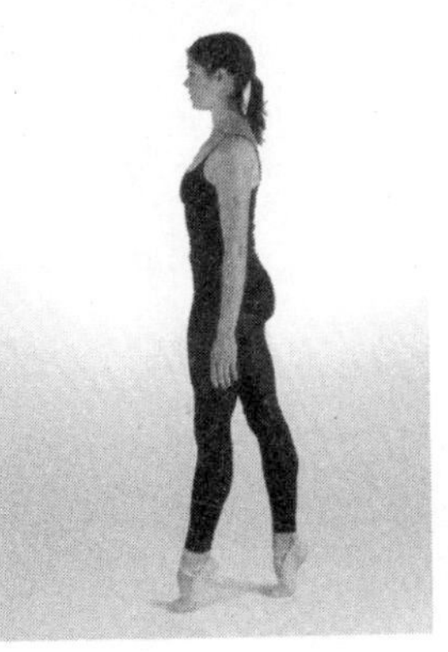

Step forward onto the demi-pointe of your left foot, then place the right foot flat onto the floor and lunge. Keep the knee directly over the toes of the foot. The thigh should be at a right angle to the floor, and the back held upright.

Lift yourself out of the lunge without letting your back drop and step straight onto the

demi-pointe of your left foot, straightening both knees. Step onto the right demi-pointe and lunge onto the left leg.

[10 reps in one direction]

[10 reps in the opposite direction]

Traveling Sautés

These jumps can also be done traveling up and down the hallway, and will really test your stamina. Remember technique is everything in jumps. Be especially careful how you land.

Begin up one end of the hallway. Stand with your feet parallel, hip-width apart, arms down by your sides.

Inhale. Bend your knees, and keep your back upright.

Exhale. Push down into the floor with your feet.

Inhale. Swing your arms forward to shoulder height to help propel you forward as you leap into the air. Straighten your knees and point your feet.

Exhale. Land working through your feet – toes, balls, heels. Bend your knees and bring your arms back down to your sides.

Keep your back upright and recruit your abdominals for the preparation, the jump and the landing. You need strength in your legs and the core of your body to jump successfully and safely.

[10 reps in one direction]

[10 reps in the opposite direction]

Coordination Work

Now that you are gathering momentum and feeling truly inspired, it's time to further challenge your coordination.

It is important to challenge the higher brain activities by learning new exercise combinations from time to time. Once you have mastered a combination so that it becomes automatic, the involvement of the decision-making center diminishes.

Dance Sequence II

This is a great exercise for sports people who need speed, agility, and explosive power.

You can stay in the hallway or if you have a large living room try performing this moving around in a large circle. Learn the sequence slowly, step by step. Once you have memorized it, try to perform the steps seamlessly for up to a minute, to get the heart rate up.

Step onto your right foot, then the left. Jump and land on the right foot. Land with a bent knee and the foot flat on the floor.

Step onto the left foot, then the right and jump off the right foot, straightening both legs in the air. At the same time, lift both arms up into the air as if you were catching a ball. Land on two feet, holding your back upright, knees bent, and heels pressed down into the floor.

Now reverse the sequence by stepping first onto your left foot, and then the right. Jump and land on the left foot. Land with a bent knee and the foot flat on the floor.

Step onto the right foot, then the left and jump off the left foot, straightening both legs as you mark the imaginary ball. Land with both feet on the floor, back upright and knees bent.

Then begin the sequence again by stepping onto the right foot first, and so on.

Once you've got the mechanics down to a fine art, try to perform 10 reps without any pauses in between the steps.

Glissade, Assemblé & Sissonne Ouverte

You are probably feeling quite worked out by now, so be careful! When your body tires, it instinctively shifts to incorporate other muscles to assist the exhausted ones. Don't let this happen. Focus on the muscle groups you are supposed to be working.

Once you've learnt the following combination, use the full breadth of the floor and show off your agility! This is your chance to feel as fleet-footed as a gazelle. When you finish one exercise, aim to move seamlessly on to the next.

Stand with your feet parallel, arms down by your sides.

Glissade

This is a gliding step.

Bend your knees, and brush and slide your right foot to the side along the floor. Keep the right leg straight and lift the foot a little way off the floor. The left knee remains bent. Then push off your left foot, and straighten both knees at the same time.

Land on your right foot with the knee bent and the left foot held out to the side.

Bring your left foot back beside the right with both knees bent.

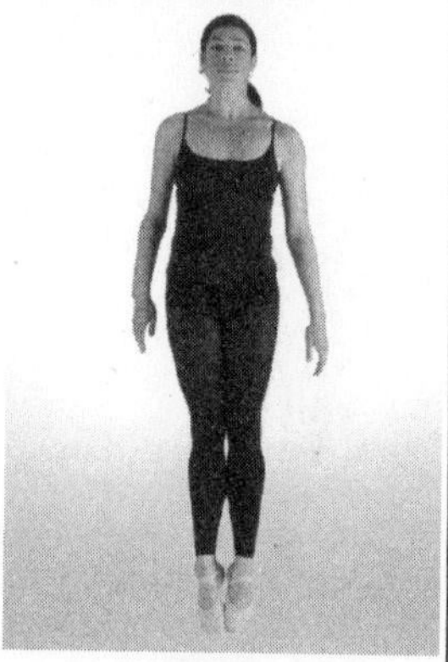

Assemblé

This is a jump from one leg, assembling both legs in the air.

Bend both knees. Brush your right leg out to the side with a straight knee and pointed foot.

Jump off your left leg and assemblé both legs in the air so that you look as if you are standing on full point in midair.

Land on the floor on two feet, heels down and knees bent. This jump does not travel, it goes straight up and down.

Sissonne Ouverte

This is a jump from two legs onto one.

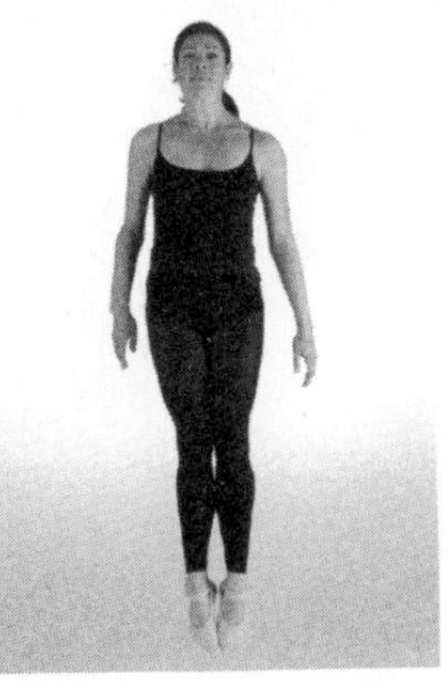

Bend both knees, and pushing through the feet, jump and travel to the right side, straightening the legs and pointing the feet.

Land on the right foot, knee bent, with your left leg still extended to the side with straight knee and pointed foot.

Push off the right foot, jump, straighten your right knee and assemblé both legs in the air.

Land on two feet with bent knees.

[8 reps alternating]

This exercise can be done from first position, with the legs turned out.

Combine the three elements, counting:

And 1 – glissade

And 2 – assemblé

And 3 – sissone

And 4 – assemblé

Alida's Tarantella

Now for the grand finale! This combination will challenge your memory, coordination and stamina.

Start with your feet together, legs parallel.

Place your hands on your hips, with your elbows to the side.

Run on the spot for 8 counts, picking up your heels.

Run in a small circle clockwise for 8 counts.

Do a small jump, landing with your feet apart, knees bent.

Jump again and bring your legs together, with your right knee turned in and bent slightly so that you can rest your right foot on the toes.

Jump back to the open position.

Jump and bring the left knee in to the right, medially rotated, and rest the left foot on the toes.

[4 reps]

Jump landing with feet apart, knees bent.

Jump onto the right leg, and swing your left leg across the body with the foot turned out and the knee bent to an angle of just more than 90 percent. Slap your left foot with your right hand.

Jump back to the open position – knees bent.

Jump onto the left leg, taking the right leg across the body and slap the right foot with your left hand.

Jump to the open position, knees bent.

Jump onto the right leg but this time swing the left leg across the back of the body and slap the left foot with the right hand.

Jump back into the open position, knees bent.

Jump onto the left leg and swing the right leg across the back of the body.

Slap the right foot with the left hand.

[4 reps, at least]

Cancan

By now your pulses should be racing. Liberating, isn't it? There's nothing like a rousing rendition of the cancan to round things off.

You can do the cancan going up and down your hallway or round and round your living room. Work up a sweat but don't exert yourself to the point where you can't speak or you experience tightness across the chest.

Start with your feet together, in parallel.

Open your arms out to the side.

Bend both knees, kick up the right leg and do a small jump on the left supporting leg at the same time. Kick the leg with a bent knee if your hamstring flexibility is limited.

Bring both legs back together and do a small jump and then kick.

Sing: together, kick, together, kick.

The trouble is that even when you are having fun, you can't sacrifice your technique if you want to benefit from this workout. So make sure you do the following:

- Do not drop your back
- Recruit your abdominals
- Hold your head erect

Cooling Down

Just as you need to prepare the body for exercise by warming up, you need to cool the body down at the end of your work-out. This will allow the accelerated heart rate to return to normal, and help the body recover.

Cooling down is the time for optimal stretching. You will notice how much more flexible you are at the end of your session, compared to how you were at the start. Hold your stretches for a few more seconds than in the warm up, and take at least 10–15 minutes to cool down and stretch out. Your body should now feel thoroughly nurtured, from top to toe, inside and out.

Adductor & Hip Stretches

To stretch the inner thigh muscles and hip flexors.

Exercise 1

Sit on the floor with your legs open as wide as you can. Make certain that you are sitting up on your sitting bones and that your lower back is lifted out of the pelvic girdle. Lengthen up and visualize a ribbon attached from the crown of your head to the ceiling. Open your arms to the side.

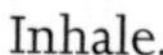

Inhale.

Exhale. Rotate your body to the right and reach down towards the right foot with your hands, keeping your spine straight. Bend forward at the hip flexors. Bring your chest down as close to your leg as possible. Slide your hands down your leg. Don't worry if you can't touch your foot; never force it. Think of melting into wet sand. Don't jerk, or you will end up shortening your muscles rather than stretching them.

Inhale. Reach further into your stretch. Hold for 30 seconds, breathing normally.

Exhale. Sit up straight and rotate your body back to the center.

Alternate sides.

[2 reps]

Exercise 2

Sit on the floor with your legs open as wide as you can. Make certain that you are sitting up on your sitting bones and that your lower back is lifted out of the pelvic girdle. Lengthen up and visualize a ribbon attached from the crown of your head to the ceiling. Open your arms to the side.

Inhale. Lengthen up through the spine and take your arms to the front at shoulder height.

Exhale. Lower your chest and arms towards the floor, keeping the spine straight. Walk your fingers along the floor to further increase the stretch.

Inhale. Reach even further into the stretch. Hold for 30 seconds, breathing normally.

Walk your fingers back, straighten your back and open your arms to the side.

[2 reps]

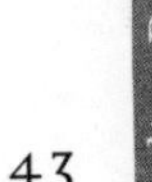

Hamstring Stretch

The hamstrings are tightened by exercise, and this stretch will help to lengthen them.

Lie on your back in constructive rest, arms resting by your sides.

Inhale. Take hold of your right leg at the thigh, calf or ankle, depending on your flexibility, and straighten the knee.

Exhale. Gently pull your right leg toward your body. Press your heel toward the ceiling and keep your buttocks firmly on the floor. Hold the stretch for 30 seconds, breathing normally.

Bend knee and repeat on the other side.

[2 reps]

If you can't reach your leg with your hands, wrap a Thera-Band or towel around your instep as an extension of your arms.

Quadriceps Stretch

This exercise stretches the muscles on the front of the thigh.

Lie on your left side with both knees bent and rest your head on your outstretched arm. Keep your hips stationary and stacked on top of one another.

Inhale. Take hold of the right foot with your upper hand, and slowly pull the foot up toward your back. Your right thigh should be parallel with the floor. Be careful not to let the upper hip roll back. Hold the stretch for 20 to 30 seconds, breathing normally.

Release the foot and then repeat the stretch.

Change sides.

[2 reps]

GLUTEI STRETCH

Glutei are the muscles that form the buttocks.

Lie on your back in the constructive rest position.

Inhale. Cross your left ankle over your right knee. Clasp your hands around the base of your right thigh. Relax and lengthen your neck and trunk.

Exhale. Recruit your abdominals and ease your right thigh in toward your chest with your hands. At the same time, press lightly into the left thigh with your left elbow. You should feel a stretch along your left buttock.

Inhale and exhale for 20 to 30 seconds, trying to draw your leg in closer to the chest on each exhalation.

Alternate sides.

[2 reps]

Large Hip Rolls

To mobilize the spine and stretch your lower back and hips.

Lie on your back, arms stretched out to the sides, palms facing down and just below shoulder level. Bend your knees and lift your legs so your thighs are at 90 degrees.

Inhale. Center your body.

Exhale. Treating the two legs as one unit, roll them over to one side of your body and rotate your head in the opposite direction.

Inhale. Bring your legs and head back to the center.

Exhale. Roll your bent knees in the other direction. Rotate your head to the opposite side.

[10 reps]

Rest Position

To stretch your back.

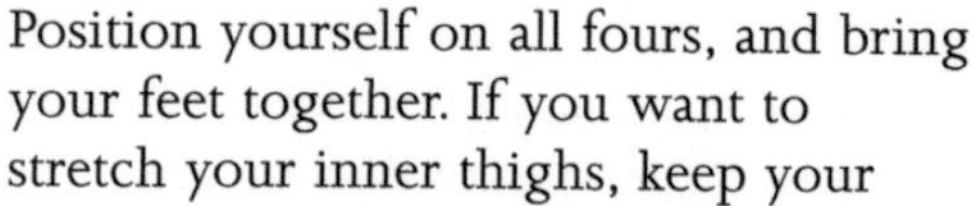

Position yourself on all fours, and bring your feet together. If you want to stretch your inner thighs, keep your knees apart. If your knees are together, the emphasis will be on a lumbar stretch.

Move your weight onto your buttocks and sit on your feet. Keep your back rounded and place your face down on the floor, arms extended.

Inhale. Feel your ribs and back expand.

Exhale. Recruit your abdominals and think of dropping your tailbone down. Hold for at least 30 seconds, breathing deeply.

Optional Wall Push-ups

Exercise 1

To strengthen pectorals and deltoids.

Stand facing the wall, approximately 24 inches (60 cm) away. Press your heels together. Lift both hands overhead and place them on the wall, about 1 meter apart.

Inhale. Lift your heels slightly off the floor. Press down into the feet.

Exhale. Lean forward and push against the wall, recruiting the abdominals so that there is a straight line from the heels to the head. Don't let the abdominals sag.

Hold for 6 to 10 seconds.

[3 to 4 reps]

Exercise 2

To strengthen the rhomboids and stretch the serratus anterior.

Stand facing the wall, approximately 24 inches (60 cm) away. Press your heels together. Lift both hands out to the side to the height of your shoulders. Press your hands against the wall.

Inhale. Bend your knees, and keeping your back lengthened, bend your elbows slightly. Lean your trunk towards the wall, and allow your heels to lift slightly while still pressing them together.

Exhale. Recruit your abdominals, stabilize your shoulder blades and push away from the wall, stretching your arms out to the sides. Make certain that your abdominals are recruited to support your back.

Hold for 6 to 10 seconds.

[3 to 4 reps]

Exercise 3

To strengthen the pectorals and the latissimus dorsi.

Stand facing the wall, approximately 24 inches (60 cm) away. Press your heels together. Lower your arms besides your body, and turn the palms of your hands towards the wall, fingers pointing to the floor.

Place your palms against the wall, keeping your shoulders open.

Inhale. Push through your feet and lift the heels off the floor. Lean forward towards the wall and bend your elbows, keeping them close to the side of your ribs. Recruit your abdominals.

Exhale. Push against the wall. There should be a straight line from your thighs to your shoulders and your body should be parallel to the wall.

Hold for 6 to 10 seconds.

[3 to 4 reps]

Exercise 4

To strengthen the triceps.

Stand with your back to the wall, approximately 8 inches (18 cm) away. Keep your feet parallel, arms down by your sides.

Inhale. Bend your knees and stretch your arms to the back, hands hip-width apart. Place your palms against the wall at hip height, fingertips pointing downwards.

Inhale. Lean into the wall as if you are pushing it away.

Exhale. Straighten your knees and keep pushing against the wall. Keep your head in line with your spine.

Hold for 6 to 10 seconds.

[4 reps]

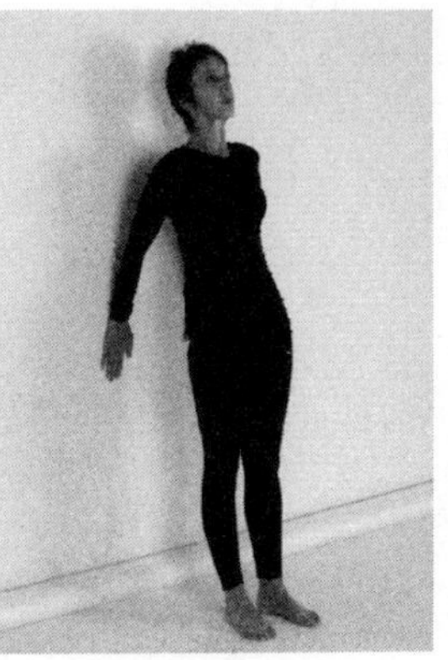

adagio: Slow dance movements.

arabesque: A position where one leg is lifted behind the body.

assemblé: A jump off one foot, assembling both legs in the air.

attitude: A position where one leg is lifted off the floor with a bent knee.

balancé: A waltz step.

barre: A long pipe-like fixture attached to the wall that ballet dancers use to support themselves while they are warming up.

chassé: A galloping step.

constructive rest: A position on the back with knees comfortably bent, feet parallel on floor, hip-width apart, and toes in the same line as legs. The back is in neutral with relaxed neck, shoulders, and head.

core stability: In Pilates the core muscles are called the powerhouse. This constitutes the group of muscles from the diaphragm to the pelvic floor including the abdominal muscles, buttock muscles, lower back muscles, and the whole pelvic function. The abdominal muscles surround and support the lower trunk and connect the pelvis to the ribs. The six-pack or rectus abdominus is the flavor of the month, but in fact it is the most superficial of all the abdominals. Pilates is much more preoccupied with the deeper stabilizing abdominals, which act as our second spine – they are the external and internal obliques that wrap themselves around the waist. The internal obliques help bend and spirally twist the trunk as well as flattening the stomach. The external obliques help with side bending, twisting, and rotation of the trunk and narrowing of the waist. The transversus abdominis forms the deepest layer and provides support to the internal organs. When contracted they pull the abdominal wall toward the spine. The four abdominal muscles form a corset from the pubic bone to the ribs and wrap around the body right to the spine. It is only when you are breathing correctly that you can activate the correct lateral and deep abdominal muscles.

dégagé: A step in which the foot is extended and lifted off the floor at an angle of 45 degrees.

demi-plié: Half a plié – a step where the knees are half-bent, with the heels remaining on the floor.

demi-pointe: Standing on the balls of your feet.

echappé: A jump from a closed position to an open one.

épaulement: A shoulder movement in which the body is twisted away from facing front, usually by $\frac{1}{8}$.

first position: A position of the feet where the heels are touching, toes pointed outward, and the knees are straight.

flex the foot: Bringing the toes of the foot up towards the body by hinging at the ankle.

fondu: A knee bend on one leg.

glissade: A gliding step.

grand battement en cloche: High kicks backwards and forwards like a bell.

hamstrings: Muscles and tendons that run up the back of the leg from the knee to the buttocks.

jeté: A jump where you brush one foot along the floor, draw a 4 in the air, and land on the other leg.

metatarsal: Five long bones in the foot.

neutral: The correct natural shape of the spine and pelvis. If the top of the pelvis tips forward, the lumbar curve increases. If it tips back, the lumbar spine flattens. Neutral is the position between the two extremes.

pelvic floor: The pelvic floor is made up of the urethra and vagina or penis and testes in front, and the anus at the back, surrounded by a band of muscle called the perineum.

petit allegro: Small jumping steps.

plié: A deep knee bend.

port de bras: Translated as "carriage of the arms", this is an arm movement from one position to another.

posé tombé: A step that involves a drop towards the floor.

pulses: Short shallow movements in time with short shallow exhalations.

recruit: To engage a specific group of muscles.

relevé: A rise onto the ball of the foot. This can be done on one foot or two, and with a demi-plié or straight knees.

retiré: A movement where one foot is drawn along the opposite leg to the height of the knee.

rond de jambe: Translated as "round of the leg", this is a step where the leg is moved in a circular motion.

sauté: A small jump from two legs landing on two.

second position: A position of the feet where they are placed slightly wider than hip-width apart, toes pointed outward. Knees are kept straight.

sissonne: A jump from two legs onto one leg.

supine: Lying on the back.

temps lié: To transfer from one position to another.

Thera-Band™: A long piece of elasticized rubber.

third position: A position of the feet where one foot is placed in front of the other, with the heel of the front foot touching the middle of the back foot. Toes are pointed outward, and knees are straight.

thoracic: The twelve thoracic vertebrae of the vertebral column articulate with the ribs.

transversus abdominis: Muscles that wrap around the abdomen in the deepest layer.

xiphoid process: A small projection at the base of the sternum.

Index